LONDON

Stephen Halliday

RYDON
PUBLISHING

A Rydon Publishing Book
35 The Quadrant
Hassocks
West Sussex
BN6 8BP
www.rydonpublishing.co.uk
www.rydonpublishing.com

Revised edition first published by Rydon Publishing in 2015
First published by David & Charles in 2011

ISBN: 978-1-910821-02-2

Printed in Great Britain by Polestar Wheatons

CONTENTS

INTRODUCTION

In 1901 London was, in a very real sense the capital city of the world. As Queen Victoria approached the end of her long reign (she died in January of that year) she reigned over the greatest empire the world had ever seen, comprising about a fifth of its surface area and a quarter of its inhabitants. 'Pax Britannica', enforced by the Royal Navy, ensured that no major international conflict on the scale of the Napoleonic Wars had taken place for almost a century. The Port of London was by some distance the busiest in the world with its forests of masted vessels bringing food and raw materials from every corner of the world and exporting manufactured goods from Britain, the workshop of the world. And the City of London, within the famous square mile that had first been bounded by its Roman Walls (still visible in many places), was the undisputed centre of world commerce and finance. In the course of a century London's population had grown from less than a million to more than six million, making it the most populous city on earth. This concentration of humanity had presented tremendous challenges to engineers, builders, social reformers and politicians who had struggled, with some success, to make London a safe place in which to live as well as a prosperous and busy one. It continued to expand up to the outbreak of World War II. Since that time the population of London has fallen as its inhabitants have moved to suburbs and new towns but although it is no longer the world's largest city it remains the one with the richest history. It is still possible, with little effort, to find traces of the city which was built by the Roman invaders and sacked by an enraged Boudicca, Queen of the Iceni, reputedly buried beneath the feet of busy travellers as they hurry along platform ten of King's Cross Station. The Roman gates of the city are still remembered in names like Aldgate (home of Geoffrey

Chaucer as he watched the Peasants' Revolt unfold in 1381) and Cripplegate, close to the lodging house of one William Shakespeare and to a small church, St Giles's, which was the scene of a turning point in which Britain fought for its life and that of the free world in 1940. And one cannot move far in London without being reminded of the personalities who made its history: Richard Whittington who helped make London the centre of the trade in wool; Thomas Gresham who ensured that London would become the financial centre which it remains in the 21st century; Prince Albert who, though his support for the Great Exhibition of 1851, left us not only the hall named after him but the Kensington museums which lie behind it. Then there is Big Ben which caused its creator so much trouble that he died prematurely and the Underground Railway which would never have been constructed without the activities of a motley crew of fraudsters, bankrupts and gaolbirds as well as a few honest men. And whatever is that strange 'London Stone' almost hidden behind a grill attached to a bank in Cannon Street, not to mention the metal tube which passes above the trains within Sloane Square Underground Station? Why, that's the River Westbourne of course. And who was John Snow who has a pub named after him just off Carnaby Street? Well, he was a teetotal doctor who found the cause of cholera. This book tells you about all these amazing people and events which helped to make London the world's most astonishing city, with a surprise around every corner.

The Stone of Brutus
The mythical ancient heart of London keeps a low profile

Opposite Cannon Street station in the City of London is a small stone behind an iron grille set into the wall of 111, Cannon Street. Until recently the premises were occupied by a Chinese bank; now they are home to a branch of WH Smith. The London Stone is easily overlooked by the casual pedestrian but this piece of limestone is at the centre of the legends which surround the creation of London. It is also known as the Brutus Stone and according to legend it was placed in London by a prince

of Trojan descent called Brutus (no relation to Julius Caesar's assassin) who fled from Troy at the end of the Trojan War. Brutus's arrival is given as 1074 BC (about the time of the likely date of the destruction of Troy). He brought with him his followers – known as Brutons or Britons – and founded the city of New Troy on the north bank of the Thames. To establish his new kingdom Brutus and his followers had to defeat a race of giants led by Gog and Magog who appear in Christian, Jewish and Islamic literature and who have since come to be associated with the defence of the City.

One of Brutus's successors as ruler of the kingdom of the Britons was King Lud who decided to rename the city after himself as Lud's Town, soon to be shortened to London, and Londinium upon the Roman occupation. By the 11th century Brutus's London stone had given its name to a district of the City, marked on maps as Londenstane. The location is recorded in the name of the first mayor of London in 1192, one Henry Fitzailwyn de Londenstane. By that time it was believed that the stone had been used by the Romans as a point from which to measure distances in miles throughout the Roman province of Britain settled in AD 43. This is plausible since the site of the stone was close to the Roman governor's palace and to Roman roads such as Watling Street (the present A5).

LONG-DISTANCE LATIN
A Roman mile was one thousand paces, a pace being two steps and measuring five feet. So a Roman mile is about 5,000 feet, slightly less than the 5,280 feet of a modern mile.

Many other legends have become attached to the stone during its long history. The poet William Blake identified it as a place of ritual sacrifice, associated with the Druids. It is one of many stones which are claimed as being that from which King Arthur drew Excalibur. It became enshrined in the history and literature of the City so that possession of the stone came to be associated with possession of the City itself. In Shakespeare's play *King Henry VI, Part II* the rebel Jack Cade, calling

himself John Mortimer, enters the stage, strikes his staff on London stone and declares:

> Now is Mortimer lord of this city. And here, sitting upon London stone, I charge and command that, of the city's cost, the pissing conduit run nothing but claret wine this first year of our reign.

This event occurred in 1450. Jack Cade's head soon found itself on a spike on London Bridge but the stone survived. The stone was a place where deals were made, oaths sworn and rituals enacted for hundreds of years. The Worshipful Company of Spectacle Makers, a City livery company which received its royal charter in 1629, was entrusted with checking the quality of spectacles made. Any found to be defective suffered the fate recorded in a document of 1671: 'broken, defaced and spoyled both glasse and frame the which judgement was executed accordingly in Canning [Cannon] Street on the remayning part of London Stone where the same were with a hammer broken in all pieces'.

The stone has been moved several times. It survived the Great Fire of

1666 and was set into the wall of one of Sir Christopher Wren's finest churches, St Swithin's. The church was destroyed by bombing in 1941 but the stone survived unscathed and was moved to its present position. Like the ravens of the Tower of London the stone's safety is linked to that of the City, an ancient myth claiming that 'So long as the Stone of Brutus is safe, so long shall London flourish.' The stone itself is a Grade II★ listed structure and, almost inevitably, a nearby pub is named after it.

BASILICA BRITANNICA

During the Roman occupation Londinium was the home of the Roman empire's largest basilica north of the Alps. It stretched south from the site of Leadenhall Market along the line of what is now Gracechurch Street almost to London Bridge.

Walls, amphitheatres and temples
What the Romans left for us

The Romans occupied London in AD 43 and left in 410 but traces of their occupation linger. Remains of an amphitheatre have been found in front of the Guildhall and the shape of the structure is marked in granite stones in the forecourt. Leadenhall Market, off Gracechurch Street, stands on the site of the Roman basilica. In 1954 the remains of a Temple of Mithras were found in the vicinity of Walbrook, dating from the time of the Roman occupation and devoted to a Persian deity. The artefacts are on show at the Museum of London and a reconstruction of the temple's foundations has been created at 11, Queen Victoria Street, close to the original excavation site. The most

Roman amphitheatre

conspicuous remnant of Roman London is the Roman Wall which was built of Kentish ragstone brought by barge from the Medway and up the Thames.

A BARGE TOO FAR

In 1962 building work in the vicinity of Blackfriars Bridge revealed a flat-bottomed barge which had sunk at its moorings carrying a cargo of Kentish ragstone which was intended for the Roman Wall. A coin dating from AD 89 and some recovered pottery enabled the barge, and the Wall, to be dated with some confidence to some time soon after AD 100. The remains of the barge and its contents are on display in the Museum of London.

The Roman Wall enclosed an area rather less than the 'Square Mile' of the medieval city. It was 6-9 feet wide and about 18 feet high, protected by a deep ditch. Parts of the wall may still be seen, notably those at Tower Hill, just outside the Underground station and those close to St Giles's Church, Cripplegate. Passage through the wall was through a number of gates which were usually closed at sunset.

Shut that gate!
The doors to the City

None of the original Roman or medieval gates through the City Wall may still be seen though their names are commemorated in many street and station names, all of them post-Roman. It is not even certain when the gates were built. Each consisted of a gap in the wall, usually protected by a portcullis and

Newgate

a fortified tower which, like that at Newgate, could also be used as a prison. These towers were often used to display portions of the dismembered corpses of criminals, especially traitors. Beginning at the north-west of the City and working clockwise the first was Aldersgate which led onto Watling Street. It was certainly built by the Romans though it takes its name from a later Saxon noble called Ealdred. Next is Cripplegate, also Roman, giving access to a substantial Roman fort sited at this point. The true origin of its name is now obscure but may derive from a legend that some cripples were miraculously cured when the body of King Edmund the Martyr (who gave his name to the town of Bury St Edmund's in Suffolk) passed through it after his death at the hands of marauding Danes in 870.

St John's Gate

John. It was at one time the home of the artist William Hogarth and of **the** **Gentleman's** **Magazine** *whose contributors included Dr Samuel Johnson, Oliver Goldsmith and the actor David Garrick who all worked here.*

WIDE ENOUGH FOR AN AMBULANCE?

This impressive gatehouse in St John's Lane, north of Smithfield, was built in the 12th century to give access to the Priory of St John of Jerusalem, ancestors of the St John Ambulance Service. It was rebuilt in the 16th century, extensively refurbished in 2010 and houses a fine museum dedicated to the Order of St

The first medieval gate we encounter is Moorgate built in 1415 by a mercer called Thomas Falconer to give access to the marshy fields ('Moorfields') just beyond the city walls. Bishopsgate is Roman, leading onto Ermine Street though it took its name from a bishop of London who rebuilt it in the 7th century. The Roman-built Aldgate (Anglo-Saxon for 'Old Gate') led to the east towards Colchester, at one time the Roman capital. For a while the gatehouse was the home of Geoffrey

Chaucer and his family when he worked as a collector of customs. In 1381 he watched the Essex men of the Peasants' Revolt as they passed through on their way to their fateful encounter at Smithfield where their leader, Wat Tyler, was stabbed by the Mayor of London, William Walworth, and the rebels dispersed.

Next, the 13th-century Postern Gate may still be seen close to the Tower of London; it remained in use until the 17th century. Nearby of course is the notorious Traitor's Gate, an entrance to the Tower from the river, built in 1279 during the reign of Edward I. It owes its name to the practice of ferrying condemned prisoners from trial in Westminster Hall to the Tower prior to their execution on Tower Hill. Billingsgate, which was a Thames wharf for fishermen, probably owes it name to a prominent local landowner. The famous fish market is first recorded in tolls regulations of 1016. The market itself moved to Docklands in 1982. There was at one time a Bridgegate which gave access to London Bridge but lay at the southern end of the bridge in Southwark as a defence

against attack from that direction. Dowgate, another water gate, stood at the point where the little River Walbrook enters the Thames.

YEOMEN WARDERS – COWS BEWARE

The Queen's Body Guard of the Yeomen of the Guard was established in 1485 as a bodyguard for King Henry VII following his victory over Richard III at Bosworth. They lay claim to being the oldest military unit in the world and attend the monarch on ceremonial occasions

A 'Beefeater'

such as investitures at Buckingham Palace when they wear a distinctive Tudor costume in red. The Yeomen Warders of the Tower of London are a separate body, created by Edward VI as gaolers at the Tower of London, where they normally reside in their distinctive blue uniforms, guiding tourists. The two bodies are often confused and referred to as Beefeaters, an expression attributed to the Grand Duke of Tuscany who described them as 'eaters of beef, of which a considerable portion is allowed them daily'.

The church of St Mary-le-Bow

The last two gates were used as prisons. Ludgate, at the foot of Ludgate Hill, despite its legendary association with King Lud, owes its name to Anglo-Saxon words meaning 'opening gate' and from 1378 was used as a prison for freemen of the City who were debtors. More serious criminals were kept at Newgate which had been used for this purpose since the 12th century. Roman in origin, the road passing through it led to important Roman towns to the west like Bath, Cirencester and Silchester. It probably owes its name to the fact that it became the principal western exit from the City during the construction of the medieval St Paul's Cathedral in the 12th century when building works obstructed the access to Ludgate.

In medieval times the gates would have been closed at dusk, this being signalled by the ringing of the bells of the church of St Mary-le-Bow.

At sixes and sevens
The City livery companies

The origins of these strange institutions are to be found in Anglo-Saxon times. In the 960s King Edgar granted a group of young men the right to use waste land in the vicinity of Aldgate in return for their services, probably in a military capacity. They were called the Cneughten Guild, the word 'cneughten' meaning young men and the word 'guild' deriving from 'geld' meaning money or payment. Edgar's grant began a long process by which the citizens of London bargained with their sovereigns, raising money for kings at a time when the machinery for collecting taxes was rudimentary. By the 12th century certain groups like the bakers had gained the right to collect taxes from amongst themselves on behalf of the king and it was becoming common for trades to be associated with certain streets or areas. These may still be detected in familiar names like Milk Street, Bread Street and Ironmonger Lane. These associations, called guilds or companies, were also beginning to administer their own rules: checking weights and measures; fixing wages and prices; defending their interests against rival bodies; and, above all, controlling entry to their professions. An apprentice had to serve a master for a period of about seven years before he could become a full member of his company or 'freeman'. The freeman survives in the 21st century, the rank being gained in one of three ways: by servitude, involving a period of apprenticeship; by patrimony, reserved for sons or daughters born while their father is a serving freeman; or by redemption, that is upon presentation by one of the City livery companies and payment of a fee.

Relations amongst companies were often strained. In 1226 the Goldsmiths engaged in a pitched battle with the Taylors. Over 500 men were involved, smiting one another with staves and swords. A sheriff had to be summoned to restore order, following which 13 offenders were hanged. In 1431 the Brewers company resolved that each member should send a barrel of ale to comfort the king's army in

France. A brewer called Will Payne, of the Swan in Threadneedle Street, refused to comply. Perhaps he was an early Eurosceptic who disapproved of foreign entanglements. Attempts at persuasion failed. He was taken before the mayor by the Master of the Brewers Company and threatened with gaol. The troops got their ale.

Apothecaries' Hall

There are now 110 livery companies, the newest being the Worshipful Company of Art Scholars, admitted to Livery in 2014. Many of them have magnificent halls, notably the Mercers in Ironmonger Lane, the Goldsmiths in Foster Lane and the Barber Surgeons in the Barbican. Their activities are now mostly social and charitable but they still play a part in the government of the City in electing the Lord Mayor and taking part in the procession which accompanies the Lord Mayor's Show each November, an order of precedence being carefully observed on such occasions.

FORTUNE FAVOURS THE PHARMACISTS

Most of the livery halls were destroyed in the Great Fire of 1666 and, having been rebuilt, were destroyed again by bombing in World War II. The exception is Apothecaries' Hall, Blackfriars Lane, which was rebuilt in 1688 and survived the Blitz. Besides being a magnificent example of late 17th-century architecture it has accommodated such famous members of the Worshipful Society of Apothecaries as Edward Jenner who introduced vaccination against smallpox, and Humphrey Davy, inventor of the safety lamp.

In 1515, following disputes amongst the livery companies, the Court of Aldermen established an order of precedence based upon the antiquity and financial strength of each. This led to the emergence of the Great Twelve which continues to the present day. They are, in order of precedence, the Worshipful Companies of:

1. Mercers
2. Grocers
3. Drapers
4. Fishmongers
5. Goldsmiths
6. Merchant Taylors
7. Skinners
8. Haberdashers
9. Salters
10. Ironmongers
11. Vintners
12. Clothworkers

The Merchant Taylors and Skinners alternate in precedence, changing each Easter, a practice which accounts for the expression at 'sixes and sevens'.

THE CITY ELDERS

As the governing body of the City, the Court of Aldermen was established by King John in 1200. It was presided over by the mayor. In 1377 the principle was established that Aldermen were elected for life by one of the City's 'wards', an arrangement which continued until 1975 when a retirement age of 75 was imposed. The role of the Court of Aldermen is now largely ceremonial though it still exercises some responsibilities in connection with the City livery companies and the City police force, which remains independent of the Metropolitan Police.

Dick Whittington
London's pantomime perennial – truth or fiction?

Richard Whittington was Mayor of the City of London three times – in 1397, 1406 and 1419 (the term Lord Mayor was not made official until 2006 though it was in common use from the 16th century). He was born in the hamlet of Pauntley, near Gloucester, in about 1359, the year his father, Sir William Whittington, died – hence the 'orphan' story which became attached to him. As a younger son he inherited little but, as was common practice at the time for the sons of the gentry, he was apprenticed to a London entrepreneur in the 1370s and soon established himself as a successful and wealthy cloth merchant. In about 1385 he married Alice Fitzwarren, the daughter of a Gloucestershire

WONDERFUL MUSEUM.

Portrait of S.ʳ RICHᵈ WITTINGTON, & his Cat. from an Original Painting at Mercers Hall.

Dick Whittington

knight, and later became a confidant of King Henry V who entrusted him with funds to pay for the rebuilding of Westminster Abbey and for improvements to the City's sewerage and water supply.

Whittington was also responsible for one of the earliest records of the City's customs and procedures. This is the *Liber Albus*, or *White Book*, which was compiled by John Carpenter in 1419. Carpenter was a lawyer who, in 1417, became Clerk to the City and was later appointed by Whittington as one of the four executors of his will. His introduction records that 'A volume of this nature, by favour of our Lord, is now at length compiled, in the Mayoralty of that illustrious man Richard Whittington, in the month of November, in the year of our Lord's incarnation 1419.' The book remains one of the most valuable sources of information about medieval London. Richard also left money for the rebuilding of Newgate prison which, until its destruction in the Great Fire of 1666, was known as 'The Whit'.

The link with the cat is harder to prove but persistent. A statue in one of the niches on the front of the rebuilt Newgate prison was reported as having a figure of Whittington accompanied by a cat – as was a portrait, now lost, in Mercers Hall. In 1946 builders carrying out restoration work in the church of St Michael Paternoster Royal discovered the mummified remains of a cat walled in behind a cornice of the tower, close to the tomb of Richard Whittington who was buried in 1423. By the terms of Whittington's will the church had been rebuilt in the 15th century. It was rebuilt for a second time by Wren following the fire of 1666 and the cat was evidently re-interred there. Perhaps the most convincing evidence of the cat legend is to be found in a museum. In 1862 some building work was undertaken on some dwellings in Westgate Street, Gloucester which are known to have belonged to the Whittington family in the 15th century. One of the buildings was found to have a bas-relief in stone which showed the unmistakable figure of a man with a cat, dating from Richard Whittington's time. This strange artefact is now a prized exhibit in the Gloucestershire folk museum.

The Highgate Hill story is harder to swallow. If, as we are encouraged to believe, Whittington was heading back to Pauntley in despair when he was summoned back by Bow Bells, then he must have had a very poor sense of direction if he passed through Highgate. There is, however, a Highgate connection since the almshouses which were established under the terms of his will were situated there until the 19th century when they were relocated to East Grinstead, where they remain.

A Tale of Two Cities
And one salmon

London is really two cities: the settlement that the Romans called Londinium and the separate community of Westminster whose name derives from its location west of the City of London. A minster was a community of clergy whose services would be offered to worshippers who did not have their own resident priests. Legend attributed the foundation of the first Westminster Abbey to Sebert, King of the East Saxons in about 616, an event supposedly attended by miraculous

London: A tale of two cities

events including the appearance of St Peter who was said to have consecrated the building himself the night before the Bishop of London was due to perform this office. St Peter also presented an undoubtedly surprised Saxon fisherman, Edric, with a miraculous draught of salmon. In memory of Edric's good fortune Thames fishermen presented a salmon to the abbey each year until the custom lapsed in 1382. In 960 King Edgar granted the abbey to St Dunstan, Bishop of London.

The Abbey of St Dunstan

A HOLY TRINITY

Three London churches have borne the name of St Dunstan. The oldest is that of Stepney, built by Dunstan himself in the 10th century. It is sometimes known as the sailors' church because it was the first church seen by ships entering the docks of London and it was the church where births at sea were registered. St Dunstan-in-the-East, in Great Tower Street, was built by Wren with a spectacular tower and spire which are all that survived the Blitz. The equally striking tower of St Dunstan-in-the-West dominates Fleet Street.

When originally built the abbey had stood on an island in the Thames called Thorney Island or the Island of Thorns. The island was formed by the delta of the River Tyburn which rises on Hampstead Heath and flows mostly underground before entering the Thames in two branches (hence the delta), one at Millbank and the other near Westminster underground Station.

Westminster Abbey owes its

prominence to Edward the Confessor (reigned 1043-1066) who was a generous benefactor and chose it as the site of his tomb. By the time of his reign the abbey was a substantial building, occupied by monks who had first been introduced by St Dunstan, while Thorney Island itself had established royal associations. Canute created the first royal residence on Thorney Island to replace a dilapidated one at Aldermanbury in the City. Edward was crowned in Winchester, the capital of Wessex, but all subsequent coronations, beginning with that of the ill-fated Harold, took place at Westminster Abbey. From 1066 Westminster was the seat of government, which it remains to this day.

Propping up the Bar
The Temple boundary

Temple Bar, first mentioned in 1293 during the reign of King Edward I, marked the boundary between the cities of London and Westminster, taking its name from the Temple church which at the time belonged to the Knights Templar but which now serves two Inns of Court, the Inner Temple and Middle Temple. It has long been a custom that a monarch, newly enthroned, stops at Temple Bar before entering the City so that the Lord Mayor can offer the monarch the City's sword of state as a token of loyalty. The sword is returned and carried before the sovereign's carriage to signify that the monarch is in the City under the protection of the Lord Mayor. In 1669, as part of the rebuilding of London after the Great Fire, King Charles I commissioned Wren to design a fine arch of Portland stone which was opened in 1672 and used to display traitors' heads impaled on spikes mounted on the top of the arch. A telescope was available at a halfpenny a time for those who wished to observe the heads more closely, and next to the Bar was a pillory. The many victims held in the pillory included Daniel Defoe, author of *Robinson Crusoe*, who was punished for a satirical pamphlet called *The Shortest Way with Dissenters*. Such was his popularity, however, that the

Daniel Defoe

crowds, instead of throwing harmful objects, garlanded him with flowers and protected him from his critics.

By 1800 all the other gateways to London had been demolished as barriers to traffic but Temple Bar survived as an obstacle on one of London busiest thoroughfares, where the Strand joins Fleet Street. In 1878, however, the City Corporation dismantled the structure and sold it to the wealthy brewer Sir Henry Meux who bought it to please his wife Valerie, a former barmaid, and re-erected it at his home, Theobalds Park, near Cheshunt in Hertfordshire. The Bar was replaced by a plinth bearing a griffin in front of the Royal Courts of Justice to mark the City boundary. The griffin, a mythical beast with the body of a lion and the head and wings of a eagle, is a traditional symbol of the City. Although visitors to Theobalds Park, who were entertained by the banjo-playing Lady Meux in the room above the arch, included Edward VII and Winston Churchill the arch became dilapidated and in 1984 it was bought by the Temple Bar Trust for £1. After further vicissitudes it was re-erected as an entrance to the rebuilt Paternoster Square, adjacent to St Paul's Cathedral where, restored, it was reopened to the public in 2004. Temple Bar is mentioned in many works of literature, notably *A Tale of Two Cities* by Charles Dickens who referred to the 18th-century sight of severed heads 'exposed on Temple Bar with an insensate brutality and ferocity worthy of Abyssinia'.

'ALL SORTS OF BOOKS'
John Stow, chronicler of London, wrote in 1600 of Paternoster Square that it accommodated 'stationers or text writers who dwelt there who

wrote and sold all sorts of books'. It remained a home of publishers until World War II when it was wrecked by bombs, some six million books being destroyed. The area's redevelopment in the 1980s aroused much controversy, the criticism being led by the architecture enthusiast the Prince of Wales.

Throw another tax record on the fire
The burning down of Parliament

In 1834 Parliament ('The Palace of Westminster') was still largely a medieval building, including the magnificent Westminster Hall, dating from the reign of William II (1087–1100) and extended by Richard II between 1397 and 1399. But in 1834 a well-meaning official of the Houses of Parliament drew attention to the large number of tally sticks, wooden receipts for tax payments dating from medieval times, stored in the cellars of the building. In an early and commendable example of recycling a decision was taken to use them as fuel in the central heating system. The ancient, rotting wood burned so merrily that most of the building was reduced to cinders though much of the stone-built Westminster Hall itself was preserved.

LYING-IN-STATE
Westminster Hall was at the heart of government in the Middle Ages and witnessed some of the most famous trials in English history, including those of Thomas More, Anne Boleyn, Guy Fawkes and Charles I. After conviction, prisoners were taken by boat to the Tower of London, entering by Traitors' Gate. Westminster Hall

Westminster Hall

Traitors' Gate

was the home of the Law Courts until they moved to the Strand in 1882. Throughout history, deceased monarchs and great statesmen have been honoured with a period of lying-in-state here before burial.

When architect Charles Barry (1795-1860) won the competition to design the new Palace of Westminster he can have had little idea of the trouble he would face in building the Parliamentary Clock. While Barry was responsible for the building itself, Edmund Beckett

Denison, first Baron Grimthorpe (1816-1905), was entrusted with designing the clockwork mechanism. Grimthorpe trained as a barrister but devoted his life to the restoration of churches in the Gothic style of which he approved, and to the design of clocks. Some idea of his talents and his temperament may be gleaned from the fact that, when he was elected as president of the Horological Institute in recognition of his expertise, it was stipulated that he

Charles Barry

be excluded from their dinners in order to avoid the arguments that would surely follow!

When Charles Barry tried to extract from Grimthorpe information about the size of the bells and other mechanisms that he had to accommodate, Grimthorpe wrote a series of offensive letters to *The Times* with headings such as 'The stupidity of Charles Barry'. The Great Bell, whose function is to sound the hours, was cast in 1856, weighed 16 tons and was hauled into place the same year. The foundry which cast the bell had specified that the clapper should not weigh more than 7 hundredweight. Grimthorpe, whose views left no room for those of others, insisted on a clapper weighing 13 hundredweight. Alas, this caused the bell to crack. It was immediately removed, recast at the Whitehapel foundry and reinstalled. It cracked again but was repaired in situ and remains cracked to this day. In the meantime the clock's hands had been redesigned. The original hands were so heavy that they ran fast to half past the hour and struggled up the clockface in their journey back to twelve!

WHO WAS BIG BEN?
The Great Clock itself is housed in St Stephen's Tower which also incorporates a prison cell to accommodate persons disrespectful to Parliament. The last occupant was the suffragette Mrs Emmeline Pankhurst, who was confined there in 1902. Big Ben is the great bell in the tower which strikes the hour. The name quickly became attached

Big Ben

to the clock but its origin is not clear. One contender is Sir Benjamin Hall, MP, Chief Commissioner of Works, who oversaw the last stages of the rebuilding of Parliament after the fire of 1834. Another tradition holds that the name was that of Ben Caunt, an 18-stone boxer known as 'Big Ben' who retired from the ring at the time the clock was completed.

Boudicca

London Calling
From Roman trading post to world capital

The first reliable estimate of London's population dates from the first annual census of 1801 when it was recorded as 949,310, the largest city in the world by a considerable margin. Contemporary records suggest that the population of London at the time of the rebellion of Boudicca (Boadicea) in AD 60 was about 30,000, by far the largest city in Britain, later growing to 50,000. The population declined after the Romans left and was probably about 25,000 in 1200. By the time of the Black Death in 1350 it had recovered to about 50,000, the same level as Roman London at its maximum and three times as large as Bristol or York, the next in size. By comparison, Paris at this time had about 200,000 inhabitants. The Black Death may have killed up to half of the population. The expansion of London gathered pace in the Tudor period, reaching 200,000 by 1600 and 600,000 by 1700. By that date London was the most populous city in Europe and probably in the world. Shortly after the dawn of the 19th century the population passed one million. By 1901 the population of Greater London was 6,501,889 and it was the principal trading and financial city of the world as well as the capital of the British Empire. The population peaked in 1939 at about 8.6 million.

After World War II much of

the population of London was rehoused in the New Towns such as Harlow, Hemel Hempstead and Stevenage which were designed to provide better living conditions than their residents had known in the slums and tenements of London, many of which had in any case been destroyed by bombing. By this time a limit to the expansion of the metropolis had been set by the creation of the Green Belt. The population of Greater London is now about 8.6 million of which 44 per cent are black or of another ethnic minority in origin.

TIGHTENING THE GREEN BELT

The first Green Belt was created by Elizabeth I who in 1580 forbade the construction of new buildings on a strip of land 3 miles wide around the City of London. In 1891 the London County Council asked Parliament to consider limiting the expansion of London but little happened until 1938 when the Green Belt Act, inspired by Herbert Morrison, gave local councils authority to buy up land in a 'girdle' about 5 miles wide around London. The new towns referred to had to leapfrog the Green Belt.

'A disgrace to civilisation'?
London and its metropolitan mayors

In November 2010 Alderman Michael Bear, a property developer from Finchley, was sworn in as the 683rd Lord Mayor of London. But his authority extends only over the 'Square Mile' of the City of London. There have been only two mayors of the whole Metropolitan area: Ken Livingstone, who was elected

Boris Johnson

twice and held the office from 2000 to 2008; and Boris Johnson who ousted him in 2008. Yet some would argue that the first Mayor of London, in fact if not in name, was Herbert Morrison (1888–1965).

Prior to 1856 London, outside the City, had no Metropolitan government. It was run by vestries, glorified parish councils, whose main aims were to keep down the rates and pass on any problems, such as sewage, to the neighbouring parish. In 1856 London acquired its first effective city-wide administration in the form of the Metropolitan Board of Works which built London's first effective sewerage system, major roads, bridges and parks. It was replaced by the London County Council (LCC), which with greater powers governed London from 1889 to 1965, its lifetime almost exactly corresponding with that of Herbert Morrison.

Born in Brixton, the son of a policeman, Morrison became a dynamic force in the London Labour Party which he virtually created in the years before and after World War I, organising such activities and fund-raising events as choirs and leagues for football, darts and cricket, explaining 'We must not only work our way to Socialism, we must sing in the course of our journey.' Elected to the LCC in 1922 he was its leader from 1934–40 by which time he was also a Member of Parliament.

He was instrumental in the creation of the Green Belt and also of London Transport which before 1933 was in the hands of a network of private companies. During World War II he was Home Secretary in Churchill's coalition government, opened the underground stations as air raid shelters and equipped them with bunks, lavatories, entertainments and refreshment trains. He enjoyed the distinction of being on the 'hit list' of Communists and Nazis because of his relentless opposition to both. He occasionally despaired of London, declaring in 1924 that 'London is an absolute disgrace to civilisation. It should never have been allowed to exist and if it could conveniently be blown up it would be better for civilisation,' but by 1958 he was admitting 'I love London Town.' When he died in 1965 his ashes were scattered on the Thames at County

Hall, headquarters of the LCC until its replacement by the Greater London Council (GLC) in that year.

Yet like many dynamic individuals he made enemies. The trade union leader and later Foreign Secretary, Ernest Bevin (1881-1951), upon hearing someone observe that Morrison was his own worst enemy, commented, 'Not while I'm alive he isn't'! Morrison's energy and commitment were sometimes combined with ruthless ambition and conspiratorial methods. His grandson is Peter Mandelson.

GOING UNDERGROUND

In November 1940, during the Blitz, Herbert Morrison announced that 'a new system of tunnels' would be excavated, linked to the London Underground Railway. Eight were built, each being entered via an entrance on the surface of

futuristic design, rather like an elaborate pillbox. Each consisted of two parallel tunnels which could accommodate 8,000 people! Seven of them were built close to stations on the Northern Line from Clapham South to Belsize Park, with one alongside the Central Line at Chancery Lane. During the war they were used as shelters and the most prominent, near Goodge Street station, was used by Eisenhower and Montgomery as an HQ for planning the invasion of Normandy. It is now used as a document store called the Eisenhower Centre. Most of the others are used for the same purpose.

London Bridge is falling* down
*burning, blowing or being pulled

The first London Bridge was built by the Romans, close to the site of the present bridge and rebuilt following its destruction by Boudicca in 60 AD. A later Saxon bridge was destroyed in 1014 in an attempt by King Aethelred ('The Unready') to frustrate the forces of the Danes who were threatening London and

London Bridge

Southwark. It is this destruction which is reputedly celebrated in the rhyme 'London Bridge is falling down'. Another bridge is recorded in 1016 when King Canute's ships sailed up the Thames to take the city and the kingdom. In 1091 the bridge was destroyed by a tornado and in 1176 a more substantial stone bridge was built in the reign of Henry II. This bridge remained in use until the 1820s. It was soon lined by houses, with a gate and drawbridge at the Southwark end for defensive purposes while the City end was decorated with the heads of traitors and other criminals.

The medieval bridge had 19 arches; from 1584 one of them was occupied by a waterwheel installed by a Dutch engineer called Peter Morice and used to pump water to conduits in the city. For this he was paid ten shillings a year, later installing wheels in two further arches. The combined effect of all this masonry and machinery was to slow down the flow of the river. In 1823–31 a new stone bridge of five arches was built by Sir John Rennie, a short distance upstream from the medieval bridge, its wider arches enabling the river to flow faster which helped to prevent it freezing. In 1967–72 the present bridge of three spans was built, Rennie's bridge being dismantled and reassembled at Lake Havasu City, Arizona. Both the 19th-century bridge and its 20th-century replacement were funded by revenue from the Bridge House Estates. These arose from properties given or bequeathed to the Corporation of London in the 12th and 13th centuries for the upkeep of the medieval bridge. The revenues are still used to maintain the four bridges which are the Corporation's responsibility: Blackfriars, Southwark, London Bridge and Tower Bridge.

NEXT CHARIOT FROM PLATFORM 10 IS FOR NORWICH

Boudicca's husband, Prasutagus, ruler of the Iceni tribe in East Anglia, had agreed with the representatives of the Roman emperor, Nero, that Boudicca would succeed him. On Prasutagus's death the governor of Britain, Gaius Paulinus, ignored the agreement, had Boudicca flogged and her daughters raped, and imposed heavy taxes on the Iceni. In the ensuing rebellion both Colchester and London were sacked before Boudicca was defeated. According to persistent legend she is buried beneath what is now platform 10 of King's Cross Station in an area formerly known as Battle Bridge.

In 1879 the Metropolitan Board of Works proposed the construction of a bridge near the Tower of London to give an additional crossing point since London Bridge, at that time the lowest crossing on the Thames, was overcrowded. It was opposed by the City on the grounds that it would impede access to the wharves which were then in the Pool of London, just downstream from London Bridge; and by the inhabitants of Southwark because it would make it too easy for Eastenders to cross the river and would therefore 'have a prejudicial effect upon the value of a large amount of property'! Despite these objections the famous 'Bascule' bridge, which could open to admit ships to the Pool of London, was designed by the architect Horace Jones (who also designed Smithfield meat market) and the engineer John Wolfe-Barry who was assisted by Henry Brunel, son of Isambard Kingdom.

The engineering is ingenious. Each bascule is a giant see-saw which requires comparatively little energy to raise it. The structure of Tower Bridge is a steel frame and the stone that we see is, in effect, cladding which was used to give the bridge its 'Gothic' appearance. It was opened in 1894, amidst much ceremony, by the Prince of Wales.

The present Hammersmith Bridge replaced the original bridge (London's first suspension bridge) in 1887. The authorities were alarmed when, in 1870, twelve thousand people crowded on to the old bridge to watch the Oxford and Cambridge boat race. Designed to carry horses and cabs it survived two attempts by the IRA to blow it up and uncomplainingly accommodated heavy goods vehicles and double-decker buses until 1997 when it was briefly closed to vehicular traffic for repair. At the same time the nearby Hammersmith flyover, built in the 1960s, was closed for the same reason. Victorian engineers built things to last! The Millennium Bridge, which opened on 10th June 2000, lasted three whole days before it was closed because of a persistent wobble which caused some pedestrians to feel sick as well as unsafe. Its structure was modified and it reopened after two years, linking Bankside with the north bank of the Thames near St Paul's.

A river runs through it (usually)
London's long-gone frost fairs

The Thames is first recorded as having frozen in AD 250 during the Roman occupation of Britain, a phenomenon recorded at regular intervals until 1814. In 1410 wheeled traffic was able to cross the river for fourteen weeks and in the winter of 1683-4 an ox was roasted on the ice as part of a Frost Fair while market stalls covered the river from Temple to Southwark. The last and greatest Frost Fair occurred in 1813-14 with a grand mall called City Road running upstream from Blackfriars. The Thames watermen, alarmed at the loss of trade, carved a channel in the ice alongside the north bank and charged twopence to ferry visitors to the merriment occurring in mid-river.

In the following half century two developments ensured that the Thames would not freeze again, but they were the work of engineers rather than global warming. The

York Gate

replacement of the 19-arch medieval London Bridge by the 5-arch structure of John Rennie in the 1820s enabled the river to flow faster. And the construction of the Victoria, Albert and Chelsea Embankments by Sir Joseph Bazalgette in the 1860s reclaimed 52 acres from the river, narrowing it so that it flowed faster through the City. To build the three embankments Bazalgette used the spoil which he had excavated during the construction of London's sewer system and from the construction of the Metropolitan Underground Railway. This is seen most clearly at York Gate, situated at the bottom of Buckingham Street, off the Strand. York Gate was once the point from which the owners of the houses of the nobility (Essex House, the Savoy, etc) stepped into their boats moored on the river. York Gate is now about 100 yards from the Thames, firmly placed in Victoria Embankment Gardens. And the Strand itself is so called because it used to run close to the river. The Thames doesn't freeze any more, because it simply runs too fast.

WHY THE SAVOY?

The Savoy takes its name from Peter, Count of Savoy in what is now Franco-Italian territory, to whom in 1246 Henry III granted the land on which the palace was built. Destroyed in the Peasants' Revolt of 1381, its chapel was rebuilt in 1510 and in 1890 it became the first church to be lit by electricity. In 1909, under the incumbency of the Reverend Hugh Chapman, vice-president of the Divorce Reform Union, it became one of the first churches in which divorced people could be remarried. It contains some fine examples of pre-Reformation stained glass.

Sir Joseph Bazalgette

Dirty old town
Bazalgette and the Great Stink

In the summer of 1858 the smell from the River Thames was so foul that Members of Parliament were unable to use rooms which overlooked the river. The reason? The sewage of two and a half million citizens was flowing into the river and not only causing the phenomenon which the press dubbed 'The Great Stink' but also polluting water supplies with poisonous bacteria. Cholera alone had killed almost 40,000 in the capital while typhoid killed Prince Albert and struck down Queen Victoria and the Prince of Wales, though both survived. And since the Thames is a tidal river the sewage never went away, being borne back and forth on the tides.

VICKY'S NAUGHTY KNICKER NICKER
Typhoid wasn't Queen Victoria's only problem. Early in her reign a boy called Edward Jones broke into Buckingham Palace three times and stole items of Victoria's underwear. He was gaoled twice and when he offended a third time he was despatched to Australia, dying in 1893 an alcoholic.

The MPs were so worried by the threat to their health that they authorised Joseph Bazalgette (1819-91) to begin work on a plan which he had been advocating for years: a scheme which would intercept the sewage and conduct it to treatment works in the Thames Estuary. From 1859-75 Bazalgette built 82 miles of main sewers, some of them larger than the Underground train tunnels, and 1,100 miles of street sewers. To accommodate the sewers and to prevent the Thames from flooding he also built the Victoria, Albert and Chelsea Embankments besides creating many streets, bridges and parks. By the time he had finished his work the Thames was once again a clean river where salmon could be found and cholera and other waterborne diseases never again threatened the capital. Bazalgette was knighted by a grateful Queen Victoria in 1874.

WH SMITH GOES GREEN

In building the Victoria Embankment from Westminster to Blackfriars Bazalgette created Victoria Embankment Gardens between the Strand and the river. Prime Minister William Gladstone wanted to appropriate the land so that he could build offices on it and use the rents thus gained to abolish income tax. WH Smith, newspaperman and Member of Parliament, organised protest meetings and petitions to thwart him. So we have WH Smith to thank for Victoria Embankment Gardens, a much-needed green space in that busy, noisy part of London. But we still have income tax!

London's eternal railway ring
Commuting to the very end

A careful examination of a map of London reveals that London's main line railway stations are built in a ring, with those north of the river being located at some distance from the main centres of business, finance and entertainment where most commuters work. Starting in the north-west with Paddington we can follow the line east through the stations north of the Marylebone Road – Euston Road – Pentonville Road – City Road. These comprise Marylebone Station, Euston, St Pancras and King's Cross, leading on to Liverpool Street and Fenchurch Street which are both just within the City. To the south of the Thames we have London Bridge and Waterloo though southern commuters were

121, Westminster Bridge Road, the former London Necropolis Station

able to penetrate the area north of the river by taking trains to Cannon Street, Charing Cross and Victoria. Why did the railway companies not build their main termini within the City itself and within Westminster for the convenience of their passengers?

There are two reasons. First, the considerable areas of land required for railway termini could be purchased much more cheaply on the northern edge of the metropolis which was still largely undeveloped. Despite the prohibitive cost of land Robert Stephenson proposed to locate the terminus of the London-Birmingham Railway at the Strand (near the site now occupied by the Savoy Hotel), while Brunel wanted the Great Western Terminus to be at Pimlico rather than Paddington. Wiser counsels prevailed and were reinforced when Parliament forbade railway works south of the Marylebone-Euston-Pentonville Roads because of the disruption caused by the proposed building works. It was for this reason that the first Underground railway was built, the Metropolitan Railway, to take passengers from Paddington, Euston,

King's Cross and later St Pancras to Farringdon, additional Underground lines being added as the years passed.

The largest and busiest railway station in London is Waterloo. Opened in 1848 as the London terminus of the London and South-Western Railway it handles 90 million passengers a year on its 19 platforms (plus the two which, until 2007, were the terminus of the Eurostar Channel Tunnel trains). Clapham Junction Station, 4 miles to the south, has more trains since it is the point at which trains from Waterloo and Victoria meet. The most extraordinary feature of Waterloo however is the now forgotten London Necropolis Station which lay adjacent to the main station and was operated by the London Necropolis Company which ran funeral trains, each carrying up to 48 coffins (first, second or third class) to one of two Woking Necropolis stations at Brookwood in Surrey. Brookwood cemetery, the largest in the British Empire, opened in 1854 to provide a burial place for Londoners, the two stations being necessary to provide separate accommodation for Anglicans and

The Euston Arch

others. The last train ran in April 1941 when bombs damaged the funeral train but the elegant façade of the Necropolis station may still be seen at Westminster House, 121, Westminster Bridge Road, SE1. The cemetery at Brookwood contains a separate burial ground for Muslims, the nearby town of Woking having Britain's oldest mosque.

Great Scott

The Euston Arch is another feature of railway history that has almost disappeared from the records. This massive arch, in the Doric style, was built as an imposing entrance to Euston station in 1837 and demolished in 1961 when the station was redeveloped. This caused much controversy, with criticism led by the poet John Betjeman. The remains of the arch were discovered, well preserved, by the architectural historian Dan Cruickshank in 1994, in the bed of the River Lea. There is a proposal to have it re-erected close to its original site for which purpose an exhibition was held at Euston in May 2015.

John Betjeman was more successful in his attempts to preserve the Midland Grand Hotel, built by George Gilbert Scott (1811–78) in the Victorian Gothic style which he also employed in the Albert Memorial. This has now been refurbished and brought back into use as a luxury hotel adjacent to St Pancras International, the terminus for Eurostar trains since 2007. At the same time the main train shed was restored. Completed in 1868 by the

The Midland Grand Hotel

engineer William Henry Barlow, it was the largest single-span structure ever designed at that time and its magnificent glass roof has been returned to its former glory, a fine testimony to its Victorian origins, providing an impressive entrance to London for passengers arriving from the Continent.

The Metropolitan Railway

Dr Cuming's 'Infernal Regions'
London's Underground railways

By the 1840s London's transport problem was dire. Streets were so congested by horse-drawn traffic that it was usually quicker to walk than ride anywhere. The situation was made worse when the ring of mainline stations began to decant their commuters to the north of the present Marylebone Road-Euston Road-Pentonville Road highway, leaving them to find their own way to the City and Westminster where they wanted to go. A proposal to build a railway beneath the streets from Paddington to Farringdon, linking mainline stations, was frustrated by difficulties in raising the money,

partly because of the activities of Leopold Redpath, an officer of the Great Northern railway, who misappropriated £170,000 set aside by the Great Northern to invest in the new railway. He spent the money on 'magnificent houses and objects of vertu' and was one of the last convicts to be transported to Australia. Despite this, and the warnings of a Dr Cuming that 'The forthcoming end of the world would be hastened by the construction of underground railways burrowing into the infernal regions and thereby disturbing the devil', construction went ahead and the world's first Underground railway, the Metropolitan, was opened in January 1863.

Most of the spoil created by building the Metropolitan Railway was taken to the banks of the Thames where it was used to create the Victoria Embankment. But some of it was taken to the fringe of the built-up area and dumped at Stamford Bridge. In 1904 the site was bought by two brothers, Gus and Joseph Mears, who adopted it as a home for their new football club, Chelsea, the mounds of spoil being used to form the first terraces. The son of Joseph, also known as Jo Mears (1905-66), was chairman of Chelsea FC and of the Football Association and helped secure the World Cup for England in 1966. The ground was extensively redeveloped in the 1990s and new all-seater stands replaced the old terraces.

ONE-WAY TICKET TO SUICIDE VIA BANKRUPTCY PLEASE

Whitaker Wright

Leopold Redpath wasn't the only criminal associated with the London Underground. Whitaker Wright (1845-1904) began to build the Bakerloo Line in 1897, went bankrupt and fled to the USA.

Extradited back to Britain, he was sentenced to seven years' hard labour and committed suicide in the Law Courts. When searched, his clothing was found to contain a revolver which evidently he had been carrying throughout the trial!

The Underground railway was successful from the start, despite the problems caused by steam trains operating underground. Amazingly, no accidents appear to have resulted from the dangerous practice of illuminating the carriages with gas lamps fed from gas held in tarpaulin bags on the roofs of the carriages, surrounded by flying sparks from the steam locomotives! The Metropolitan Line was built by the 'cut and cover' method: dig a trench along a road; build the railway; fill in what remains of the trench. Later lines swiftly followed, most of them being the

An electric locomotive

'Tubes' constructed far beneath the streets using tunnelling shields. The first of these, the City and South London Railway, opened in 1890 between Stockwell and the City. It is now the southern part of the Northern Line. It was the first to use electric locomotives.

Marc Brunel's tunnel shield

MARC BRUNEL MAKES THE EARTH MOVE FOR PEDESTRIANS

Sir Marc Brunel (1769-1849), father of Isambard, devised the tunnelling shield to build the world's first tunnel beneath a river which opened between Wapping and Rotherhithe in 1843. Its iron frame protected the workmen, known as miners, from falling debris. Designed for pedestrians, the tunnel he built by this method now accommodates the East London line of the Underground. All subsequent tunnelling shields, including that used to build the Channel Tunnel, are developments of Marc Brunel's design.

The original map icon

Under the guidance of Frank Pick (1878-1941) the Underground also became known for modern, innovative design. Many of the stations on the system, notably the northern section of the Piccadilly Line, are listed buildings. Posters promoting travel were commissioned from artists who later became famous like Paul Nash and Mabel Lucie Attwell. A new typeface for station signs was commissioned from the artist Edward Johnston, sculpture from Eric Gill and Jacob Epstein and, of course, the famous Underground Map. Devised by electrical draughtsman Harry Beck (1901-74) during a period of unemployment, it was at first rejected as too

Arnos Grove station

revolutionary but is now an icon of industrial design, often imitated but never equalled.

COMRADE PICK, CAPITALIST SOVIET HERO

By the 1930s London's Underground railway was the model for other urban transport systems. Nikita Khruschev sent a delegation to London to study the network while he was building the Moscow Metro (with forced labour). The managing director of the Underground, Frank Pick, was awarded the Honorary Badge of Merit of the Soviet Union by Stalin – an unusual distinction for a director of what was then a private enterprise!

An ambling horse
The origin of the Hackney carriage

The Underground railway was not, of course, London's first public transport. That was the brainchild of a retired sailor called Captain Baily who, from about 1640, was hiring out from the Maypole Inn in the Strand *coches haquenée*, a French term for a coach pulled by an ambling horse (abbreviated to 'hack' in English). The service was so successful that the coaches were soon blocking London's narrow streets but in 1654 Oliver Cromwell licensed the Fellowship of Master Hackney Coachmen. In return for an annual licence fee of £5 the Hackneys enjoyed a monopoly of four-wheeled transport north of the Thames as far as the New Road, which is now the line of the Marylebone Road-Euston Road-Pentonville Road. Is this, perhaps, the origin of the legendary London cabbie's claim 'I don't go south of the river'? In 1694 some ladies hired a Hackney coach and took it to Hyde Park where they 'behaved disgracefully and insulted some very distinguished people driving in their private coaches'. As a result Hackneys (and their successors)

were banned from Hyde Park until 1924.

In 1823 David Davis, a resident of Mount Street, Mayfair, introduced a cabriolet: a one-horse, two-seater design from France. Painted a distinctive yellow and black they were soon known as cabs. In 1850 the Metropolitan Police assumed responsibility for the Hackneys, issuing licences and administering the fearsome Knowledge test which has survived the advent of sat-navs. Aspiring taxi drivers may be seen in London at weekends, usually on bicycles, travelling slowly around the capital memorising street names from lists mounted on handlebars. Taximeters (a French word meaning 'tariff meter') were introduced in 1907. There are now about 21,000 licensed taxis and although they are often referred to as 'black cabs' they now come in all colours.

Cabbies' cabins

Cabmen's shelters are also a distinctive feature of the capital. Made of wood, usually painted green and emitting a distinctive smell of coffee they provide refreshment stops for taxi drivers. They owe their origins to the Earl of Shaftesbury who in 1875 created the Cabmen's Shelter Fund which constructed 61 shelters, all within six miles of Charing Cross and in places frequently used by taxis. Thirteen of these survive in locations such as Russell Square, Temple Place and Hanover Square. They are all listed buildings.

DR DUNCAN – DRUNK ATTENTION SEEKER OR THE RIPPER?

In October 1888, the **Daily Telegraph** *carried an account of a visit by a mysterious stranger to the cabmen's shelter in Westbourne Grove which has since been demolished. The cabmen were discussing the latest Whitechapel murder which had taken place that morning when the stranger assured them that he was indeed the murderer. Having been invited to sign the Visitors' Book he did so as 'J. Duncan; doctor; residence, Cabman's Shelter; Sept. 30, 1888.' He then vanished, clasping the bottle of brandy that he had brought with him.*

From hearses to Bendies
London's buses

London's first bus service opened on 4th July 1829 from Paddington Green to the Bank of England. It was the brainchild of George Shillibeer (1797–1866), a coachbuilder who had visited Paris and seen the Omnibus (Latin 'for all') service introduced by Stanislas Baudry. Baudry drowned himself in the Seine when his enterprise failed, an event which foreshadowed the fate of Shillibeer's own service. The novelty of shared urban transport, together with the fearful congestion of London's streets, meant that few were attracted by the service which charged the considerable fare of a shilling (5p) for 'outside' passengers and one shilling and sixpence (7.5p) for 'inside' passengers. Shillibeer went

bankrupt, fled to Boulogne to escape his creditors and, after a short spell in a debtors' gaol, finally achieved prosperity by redesigning the vehicle as a hearse.

In the 1840s Thomas Tilling introduced an omnibus service in Peckham and in 1855 the London General Omnibus Company, with many French investors and directors involved, was established using horse buses which remained in use on London's streets until 1916. The first motor bus entered service in 1897 and in the years following World War I anarchy prevailed as 'pirate' buses, operated by independent owners, competed with the London General Omnibus Company (by now owned by the Underground Railway Group) on the most lucrative routes. The situation was resolved by the creation by Herbert Morrison in 1933 of the London Passenger Transport Board, which assumed control of all rail and road transport services within London. These included London's tramways which continued to operate until 1953.

The Parisian Omnibus

- 47 -

One famous conductor was André Previn...

In 1956 London Transport introduced the iconic Routemaster bus which was boarded via an open platform at the rear. Robust, reliable and painted red, the Routemaster became a much-loved feature of London's streets. Such was its international celebrity that it was adopted in cities in Australia, New Zealand, Canada, Alaska and China, mostly as a means of transport but also for other purposes such as hot dog stands and mobile shops. The main disadvantage of the Routemaster was that it required two crew – a conductor as well as a driver – and was largely inaccessible to wheelchairs. Services began to be withdrawn in 2003 to be replaced by driver-only vehicles with sliding doors. The last Routemaster service in London ran in December 2005. The Routemaster has now given way to the Bendy Bus, a single-decker of two conjoined sections much reviled by the mayor Boris Johnson who ran a competition for a replacement Routemaster design. True to his word, Boris withdrew the last bendy in December 2011.

LONDON'S SCARIEST MODE OF PUBLIC TRANSPORT

Since June 2012, London has seen cable cars carrying people in gondolas 50 metres above the Thames between Greenwich Peninsula and the Royal Docks at a cost of £3.40 with an Oyster Card. One of the first passengers was Boris Johnson, who distinguished himself by becoming marooned halfway across the river. He revelled in the experience. The first cable car, built with a tunnelling shield, was the Tower Subway which opened in 1870 between Tower Hill and Pickleherring Street, close to the present mooring site of the World War II cruiser HMS Belfast. Passengers paid a penny to be drawn in cable carriages beneath the river, pulled by a steam engine. Never a success, the subway still exists and is used to convey water and power lines beneath the river.

Rhyming slang and Bow Bells

How to tell if you're a proper Cockney

The term 'Cockney' derives from 14th-century English and means 'Cock's egg': an ironical reference to small or misshapen eggs laid by young hens. It was a pejorative term used by countrymen to describe supposedly weaker-bred city folk and came to refer specifically to Londoners though it has long since

St Mary-le-Bow

lost its pejorative associations and now refers to Londoners and their modes of speech. A Cockney is traditionally one who is born within the sound of the bells of the church of St Mary-le-Bow which is in Cheapside, half way between the Bank of England and St Paul's Cathedral and thus in the heart of the 'Square Mile' of the City. Thus a Cockney is strictly speaking one born within the City itself – a rare phenomenon since few families live in the City and the only hospital within the City is St Bartholomew's which has no maternity unit!

In practice the term Cockney is extended to anyone who might just, with acute hearing, be able to detect the bells when the wind is in the right direction and thus encompasses those born in Tower Hamlets. True Cockneys value their heritage and are easily offended when others from further afield (for example Hackney and Bermondsey) are honoured with the title.

Cockney rhyming slang originated in the East End of London in the early 19th century, especially amongst costermongers (market traders and barrow boys like the characters from

Only Fools and Horses). It is a form of coded language which is understood by those using it but not by others (such as policemen and market inspectors!) whose attentions were not welcomed. A few examples are:

Dog	Dog and bone	phone
Boat	Boat race	face
Loaf	Loaf of bread	head
Brown	Brown bread	dead
Trouble	Trouble & strife	wife
Butcher's	Butcher's hook	look

Some of these expressions have passed into general usage. Thus 'Use your loaf' means 'Use your head (brains)'; and 'Have a butcher's' means 'Have a look'. The vocabulary continues to grow. Recent additions make reference to TV presenter Emma Freud (haemorrhoid); a ten pound note or 'tenner' is an 'Ayrton' (Senna, a deceased Brazilian racing driver); and beers are 'Britneys' (Spears).

Crofty designs

Pearly Kings and Queens originated in London in the late 19th century amongst East End costermongers who decorated their garments with pearl buttons, different patterns

Pearly King

having meanings such as good luck (a horseshoe) or hope (an anchor). The Pearly Kings' and Queens' Association dates from 1911 and is associated with an orphan called Henry Croft (1862-1930) whose work as a roadsweeper in the East End enabled him to collect many pearl buttons which had fallen from clothing. These he used to decorate his own clothes and, with similarly accoutred costermongers, collected money for a variety of charities, notably orphanages and hospitals. A suit can hold tens of thousands of buttons and weigh as much as 30 kilograms. Henry died in 1930, his funeral being attended by 400 Pearly Kings and Queens and filmed by Pathé News. His statue is in the crypt of St Martin-in-the-Fields, Trafalgar Square. Pearly Kings and Queens are most likely to be seen on the streets at times of national celebration like royal weddings.

A dish associated with the East End is jellied eels, a cheap and nutritious food which was readily available (in its raw state at least) from Thames nets in the vicinity of London Bridge. It consisted of eels, chopped and boiled in stock and cooling to form a jelly. The first eel pie and mash houses opened in London in the 18th century and the oldest surviving one, Manze's of Bermondsey, has been trading since 1902. Eels disappeared from the Thames when it became polluted in the mid-19th century and again in the mid-20th century. Luckily for them the Thames is once again clean enough to accommodate eels and nets are allowed as far upstream as Tower Bridge, so perhaps jellied eels are ready to stage a comeback.

At home with saints and sinners
Crosby Hall's colourful occupants

In Danvers Street, Chelsea SW3, overlooking the Thames is a medieval building whose first home was the City of London. This is Crosby Hall, built in Crosby Place, Bishopsgate, for the wealthy grocer Sir John Crosby in 1475. In 1483 it was the home of Richard, Duke of Gloucester, shortly to become Richard III and, according to Shakespeare's thoroughly biased account, a blackguard whose victims included the princes in the Tower. His murderous career began when he ordered the execution of his brother the Duke of Clarence. In Shakespeare's play he addresses the murderers thus:

When you have done, repair to

Crosby Hall

Crosby Place.

But, sirs, be sudden in the execution, Withal obdurate, do not hear him plead; For Clarence is well-spoken, and perhaps may move your hearts to pity if you mark him.

Clarence was duly drowned in a barrel of Malmsey wine. In 1532 Crosby Hall became the home of Sir Thomas More, canonised in 1935, four hundred years after his execution by Henry VIII for opposing the king's break with Rome. In 1908 the site was bought by an Indian bank. Gordon Selfridge wanted to move Crosby House to the roof of

Sir Thomas More

his Oxford Street department store but instead it was dismantled and moved to the site of Thomas More's other home in Chelsea where it was re-erected as a hostel for university women. In 1989 it became the home of a successful businessman. Its magnificent hall, with hammerbeam roof, contains one of Holbein's portraits of Saint Thomas More.

London's burning... again
Women with full bladders on alert

Every Londoner has heard of the Great Fire of 1666 which began on 2nd September and spread rapidly despite the disdainful comment of the Lord Mayor that 'A woman might piss it out.' It burned for three days, destroyed 400 acres of the City and was eventually halted through determined action by Charles II and his brother, the future James II, who used gunpowder to create fire breaks. The Monument to the Great Fire was designed by Sir Christopher Wren in Portland Stone and unveiled in 1677. Two hundred and two feet high, it is still the tallest isolated stone

The Golden Boy of Pye Corner

column in the world and is situated on the site of Farriner's Baking House, Pudding Lane, where the fire began in an unquenched grate. An inscription on the Monument blamed the fire on a 'Popish frenzy, which wrought such horrors'. These last words were finally deleted in 1830 as a result of a campaign by the City Solicitor, Charles Pearson, who also campaigned for the construction of the Metropolitan Underground Railway. A less well-known monument is the Golden Boy of Pye Corner, a small monument located on the corner of Giltspur Street and Cock Lane in Smithfield, which marks the point where the fire ended. Underneath the figure of a small, stout boy is the following inscription: 'The boy at Pye Corner was erected to commemorate the staying of the Great Fire which, beginning at Pudding Lane, was ascribed to the sin of gluttony when not attributed to the papists as on the monument and the boy was made prodigiously fat to

enforce the moral.' Only six deaths from the fire were verified, one of them being the maid of the baker as she was too timid to escape with Farriner's family over the rooftops. Many deaths were probably not recorded.

CLEOPATRA'S NEEDLE

London's other freestanding monument is Cleopatra's Needle which in reality pre-dates the Egyptian queen by almost 1,500 years. Given to England by the ruler of Egypt in 1819 it was not brought to England from Egypt until 1877, when it was transported in a specially designed cylindrical pontoon which almost sank in a gale in the Bay of Biscay in which six seamen lost their lives. It was erected on the Victoria

Raising Cleopatra's Needle

Embankment in 1878 above a time capsule which contains a copy of Bradshaw's Railway Guide, a set of morning newspapers, a Bible and, oddly, pictures of 12 attractive women.

Where the Great Fire burned for three days in the 17th century, the lesser-known Great Bishopsgate Fire of 1964 burned for seven days. On 5th December the London Fire Brigade was alerted to a fire at the British Railways Bishopsgate Goods Depot near Liverpool Street. Two hundred and thirty-six men and 61 appliances were used to extinguish the blaze and were finally removed from the scene on 12th December, a week later. Two people died and Liverpool Street Station was closed for a week. A coroner's enquiry established that the fire had probably been started deliberately, possibly to conceal theft from the goods at the depot. Nothing was ever proved.

St Giles takes one for team GB
Poets, martyrs, bombs and the turning point of the Battle of Britain

In Fore Street, Cripplegate, is one of London's most amazing churches, almost lost amidst the brick, glass and steel of the Barbican. John Foxe, author of *Foxe's Book of Martyrs,* is buried here as are the Elizabethan explorer Martin Frobisher and the poet John Milton. Oliver Cromwell, who appointed Milton to the post of Secretary of Foreign Tongues while he was Lord Protector, was married in this little church and the children of Edmund Shakespeare were baptised here. A long tradition holds that Edmund's brother, William

St Giles's Church

Shakespeare, acted as their godfather and this legend gained strength in 2007 when it was learned that in 1604 William was lodging with a Huguenot family called Mountjoy in Silver Street, nearby, within the parish of St Giles. Another worshipper at the time was Sir Thomas Lucy, who is buried in the church and who was satirised by Shakespeare as Justice Shallow in *The Merry Wives of Windsor* following a poaching incident by William in Lucy's deer park near Stratford-upon-Avon.

But perhaps this little church's greatest claim to a place in history lies not with poets but with bombs. On 24th August 1940 a German bomber became lost at night over southern England. The Luftwaffe had been ordered to attack Royal Air Force (RAF) stations to eliminate the RAF in preparation for the planned German invasion – but had been forbidden to bomb London. By this stage in the Battle of Britain the RAF was severely stretched. Believing that he was over open country, the German bomber pilot jettisoned his bombs and turned for home. The bombs fell on St Giles's

Church, Cripplegate. The pilot was disciplined for his error by Luftwaffe commander-in-chief Hermann Göring. Prime Minister Winston Churchill ordered an immediate retaliatory raid on Berlin which did little damage but so enraged Hitler that he ordered the Luftwaffe to attack London instead of the RAF stations. London suffered in the Blitz that followed but the RAF could hardly believe its luck. This was a turning point. The RAF took advantage of the respite to recover, and was able to attack the Luftwaffe with renewed strength. Within three weeks the air battle was won and the planned German invasion postponed indefinitely. The church, which lies close to a large section of the remaining Roman Wall, was extensively restored after the war.

London smog
'Nobody is healthy in London, nobody can be'

In his ode 'Composed Upon Westminster Bridge, September 3rd 1802', William Wordsworth wrote of London as 'All bright and glittering in

William Wordsworth

the smokeless air'. But by 1819 his fellow poet, Shelley, wrote:

'Hell is a city much like London A populous and a smoky city'.
London smog arose in the days before smokeless fuel as a mixture of smoke and the fogs that swept through the capital. Most homes had coal-burning fires which emitted copious quantities of smoke and to this was added smoke from industry. Steam locomotives were a leading culprit; though romantic and much admired they were also serious pollutants. London smog was recorded in the novels of Charles Dickens and the adventures of Sherlock Holmes. The

French writer Hippolyte Taine wrote that 'no words can describe the fog in winter. There are days when, holding a man by the hand, one cannot see his face'. At this time Horseguards Parade was covered in a thick layer of soot and frantic efforts were made to clean up the capital before the opening of the Great Exhibition of 1851. Punch wrote that 'Every street is either whitewashing its face or rubbing up its dingy complexion with a fine layer of London cement.'

The situation in the Metropolitan Underground Railway was particularly dire. Special steam locomotives had been designed to minimise the escape of steam into the tunnels but they were not very effective and did nothing to reduce the smoke. The results were recorded in a letter to *The Times* in 1887 written by RD Blumenfeld who was to become editor of the *Daily Express*. In his diary he wrote: 'I had my first experience of Hades today and if the real thing is to be like that I shall never again do anything wrong. I got into the Underground Railway at Baker Street. I wanted to go to Moorgate... the smoke and the sulphur fill the tunnel. The atmosphere was a mixture of sulphur, coal dust and foul fumes so that by the time we reached Moorgate Street I was near dead of asphyxiation and heat. I should think these underground railways must soon be discontinued, for they are a menace to health.' Blumenfeld's pessimism was mistaken which was fortunate since his son, Sir John Elliot, became chairman of London Transport in the 1950s. A Committee of MPs was not reassured by the evidence of the Metropolitan Railway company that employees suffering from lung conditions like bronchitis and tuberculosis had been cured by exposure to the smoke; or by a train driver who told them of his excellent health after 34 years' service, even when he added that the smoke was seldom so thick as to render the signals invisible!

Smog for sale!

In 1875 the Public Health Act specified that factories should consume their own smoke 'as far as may be practicable'; a well-intentioned but ineffective call to arms. In the 1950s it was possible for visitors to the capital to buy tins of London Smog from gift shops to take home as souvenirs. The problem reached its climax with the Great Smog of 1952. This combination of smoke, fog and vehicle exhaust fumes killed 12,000 people in London alone and prompted the Clean Air Act of 1956 which banned the use of certain polluting fuels, promoted the use of smokeless fuel and banned black smoke. Eventually London could breathe again.

CHOOSE YOUR POISON: FROM HORSE MANURE TO CARBON MONOXIDE

In the 1890s London had 11,000 cabs and 1,000 omnibuses pulled by 50,000 horses. **The Times** *estimated that in 50 years every street in London would be buried under nine feet of manure. Conferences pondered the problem but were abandoned when no-one could think of a solution. Respite came from an unexpected quarter. In 1889 Gottlieb Daimler installed an internal combustion engine in a carriage. Nineteen years later Henry Ford*

*launched the Model T Ford. In 1916
London's last horse-drawn omnibus
withdrew from service. Horse
droppings in the streets were replaced
by carbon monoxide fumes in the air:
a problem yet to be overcome.*

1851 – a great year for exhibitions

The Prince and the 'most generally unpopular man'

By 1850 exhibitions to celebrate national achievements in industry, art and other fields were becoming popular. The Great Exhibition of 1851 in Hyde Park, however, was the first international exhibition. The idea is generally credited to Albert, Queen Victoria's Prince Consort but it was in reality the brainchild of Henry Cole (1808-

The Great Exhibition

82) who put the idea to the Prince after visiting the Paris Exhibition of 1849. Cole had already made a name for himself working with Rowland Hill in the introduction of the Penny Post in 1840, been responsible for the design of the famous Penny Black postage stamp and invented Christmas cards in 1843. Although Albert nominally presided over the committee that organised the Great Exhibition Henry Cole was its moving spirit, cajoling, chiding and bullying builders and exhibitors so that he became, in the words of the Prime Minister Lord Derby, 'the most generally unpopular man I know'. Recognising that behind the bullying exterior lay a dynamic personality, Albert coined the phrase 'We must have steam, get Cole.'

The problem of creating a pavilion for the exhibition in Hyde Park seemed insuperable and the very idea attracted the scorn of *The Times* which protested that it would turn Hyde Park into 'a bivouac of all the vagabonds of London'. Almost 250 designs for the pavilion were submitted to and rejected by the committee, including one from

Isambard Kingdom Brunel which would have required a year's supply of bricks and been impossible to dismantle. Sir Joseph Paxton's (1803-65) Crystal Palace design, sketched on a piece of blotting paper during a dull meeting, proposed a prefabricated structure made from standardised glass panels in a frame of cast iron components. It was so revolutionary that the organisers of the Exhibition were able to charge spectators to watch it being assembled in Hyde Park. Six times the size of St Paul's Cathedral it dominated the southern side of Hyde Park (roughly where Rotten Row is now) and defied doomsayers who predicted that it would collapse when the choir sang the Hallelujah Chorus at the opening ceremony presided over by the Queen. Almost 14,000 British and foreign participants displayed 112,000 exhibits to 6,039,195 visitors, almost as many as visited the Millennium Dome in 2000.

First time with diarrhoea and a bent penny...

Besides viewing such exhibits as early American tractors, Swiss watches and peacock feathers, visitors consumed almost 2 million buns and over a million bottles of soft drinks from a little company called Schweppes. Using a water closet for the first time was a novelty for 827,000 visitors, paying a penny each and thus adding the phrase 'spend a penny' to the language. The Exhibition was a financial success as well as a great public spectacle. A profit of £186,437 (multiply by 1,000 for the modern equivalent) was spent in beginning to create the Kensington Museums. Henry Cole was the first director of what soon became the Victoria and Albert Museum (voted Britain's favourite visitor attraction in 2010) and he was knighted in 1875, becoming known as 'Old King Cole'. The area, noted for its fine collection of museums which now include the Natural History Museum and the Science Museum as well as Imperial College and the Royal Albert Hall, became known as Albertopolis, after the late Prince.

London's park for children

Thomas Coram and the Foundling Hospital

At Brunswick Square, Bloomsbury, just north of Great Ormond Street Hospital for Children is a large park which can only be entered by adults who are accompanied by a child. We owe this to Thomas Coram (c.1668-1751) who was born in Lyme Regis and worked for 30 years as a sea captain, trading with the North American colonies. By 1720 he had retired and was living in Rotherhithe where he was frequently distressed by the sight of babies abandoned by their mothers often, literally, on heaps of rubbish. Coram drafted a petition to secure a royal charter for a foundation 'to prevent the frequent murders of poor miserable infants at their birth and to suppress the inhuman custom of

Thomas Coram's park for children

exposing new-born infants to perish in the streets'. He spent 16 years from 1721 lobbying for the required political and financial support for his 'Hospital for the Maintenance and Education of exposed and deserted young Children', and on 17th October 1739 he was granted a charter for 'an Hospital for the Reception, Maintenance and Proper Education of such cast off Children and Foundlings as may be brought to it'. He spent most of his own money and raised more from subscribers. The artists William Hogarth and Sir Joshua Reynolds donated many pictures to what became London's first picture gallery. Many of these may still be seen in the Foundling Hospital Museum in Brunswick Square. The composer Handel conducted an annual performance of *The Messiah* to raise funds.

In the 20th century, author JM Barrie was an admirer of the foundation and requested that some Coram Children attend the first performance of *Peter Pan*. He was confident that the infectious laughter of youngsters would influence the primarily adult audience's reception of the unusual story and he was correct. The first night was consequently a resounding success. Royalties on *Peter Pan* were left to Great Ormond Street Hospital.

On 24th March 1741, the trustees of the Foundling Hospital announced that 'To-morrow, at eight o'clock in the evening, this house will be opened for the reception of twenty children... no questions whatever will be asked of any person who brings a child.' Those bringing children to the hospital were requested to 'affix on them some particular writing, or other distinguishing mark or token' as some means of identification. The tokens, a collection of which remains in the possession of the Foundling Hospital Museum, included coins, trinkets, a lottery ticket, pieces of ribbon and, occasionally, poems like the following, number 5,312, deposited on 2nd August 1757:

'Here I am brought without a name
Im' [sic] sent to hide my mother's shame
I hope you'll say Im' not to Blame'
The trustees purchased land at Brunswick Square which was

occupied from 1745 and remained the home of the hospital until it was moved to Berkhamsted, Hertfordshire, in 1935. The charity itself is now known as the 'Coram Family'. Since 1955 parentless children have been fostered or adopted rather than accommodated in children's homes but the charity continues its work. It works with vulnerable children and sponsors research projects into the welfare of children.

Not all named Moses

On 2nd June 1756 the hospital began the practice of leaving a basket suspended at the entrance to the hospital. The foundling was left in the basket, the mother rang the bell and departed, leaving her infant with its 'distinguishing mark or token' to add to the hospital's growing collection. On the first day 117 children were left in the basket.

Since the children were nameless they were often given names like William Shakespeare, Geoffrey Chaucer and Francis Drake. All the children were inoculated against smallpox and a doctor attended in the case of any illnesses which could not be treated by the resident nurse. In the 19th century Charles Dickens lived nearby in Doughty Street and in March 1853 in his journal *Household Words* Dickens wrote 'this home of the blank children is by no means a blank place… the Governors of this charity are a model to all others'. Thomas Coram died on 29th March 1751, probably aged 83, and his tomb is to be found at St Andrew's, Holborn, at the southern end of Hatton Garden. Brunswick Square remains the home of the Foundling Museum with its fine collection of paintings and Foundling tokens. Outside the museum stands a statue of Thomas Coram. In 1852 the Great Ormond Street Hospital for sick children was built on neighbouring land. The adjacent land – 'Coram's Fields' – is the park which can be entered by adults only if they are accompanied by a child.

Sub judice in absentia
The lost Inns of Court

Most Londoners know of the four Inns of Court: Lincoln's Inn, Gray's Inn, the Middle Temple and Inner Temple. They date from the 14th century, possibly earlier, the word 'Inn' referring to a building in which barristers and those learning to practise the law were accommodated. Each of the Inns of Court, whose gardens are open to the public, resembles an Oxbridge college, consisting of staircases which accommodate the 'chambers' of barristers. Anyone wishing to practise as a barrister must be accepted by an Inn of Court, follow a course of study, pass examinations and then be taken on by one of the chambers. Each student also has to attend a certain number of formal dinners in the magnificent dining hall of his or her Inn. That of the Middle Temple contains a long table made from a single oak tree given to the Inn by Queen Elizabeth I and a cupboard made from the timbers of the *Golden Hind*, in which Sir Francis Drake circumnavigated the world in 1577-80.

There used to be many more Inns, known as Inns of Chancery which specialised in preparing writs for all the sovereign's courts. They have all gradually closed or been taken over by one of the four remaining Inns of Court but some buildings survive. Barnard's Inn (1435), situated in a passage off the south side of Holborn, became the site of Mercers' School in 1892 and is now the home of Gresham College. Clifford's Inn (1480) was the home of Leonard and Virginia Woolf but is recalled now only by Clifford's Inn Passage. Clement's Inn (1480), remembered by the road of that name running north of the Strand to the west of the Law Courts, was the Inn of Shakespeare's Justice Shallow.

THE VIRGIN QUEEN'S INDEPENDENT FINANCIAL ADVISOR

Sir Thomas Gresham (c.1518–79) was a City merchant who managed the finances of Elizabeth I's government. He coined the expression 'bad money tends to drive out good': in other words people will hoard sound currencies and gold coins and spend fake or debased coins and currencies which are losing value. It remains the classic argument against inflation. In 1566 he founded the Royal Exchange, thus laying the foundations for London's pre-eminence as a centre for trade and especially for finance. His will endowed Gresham College which continues to flourish in the 21st century as a provider of free public lectures by eminent scholars on every subject.

Doctors dissolved

Doctors' Commons was the name given to a college (an Inn of Court in all but name) which housed advocates who were qualified in Civil Law (i.e. non-criminal law). Based in Paternoster Row, near St Paul's Cathedral, they practised in the Court of Arches which sat originally in the church of St Mary-le-Bow, Cheapside and dealt with matrimonial matters. Doctors' Commons advocates also dealt with matters of maritime law and international trade, the most eminent being (later Sir and Saint) Thomas More who was admitted to Doctors' Commons in 1514. By the 19th century Doctors' Commons was regarded as outdated and slightly absurd, and was lampooned by Dickens in *David Copperfield* where he described it as a 'cosey, dosey, old-fashioned, time-forgotten, sleepy-headed little family-party'. Changes in the legal system led to the dissolution of Doctors' Commons in 1865 and the sale of its buildings, which had by then been relocated to Knightrider Street. The buildings and the street were demolished in 1867. The former site of Doctors' Commons is now marked by a plaque on the Faraday Building on the north side of Queen Victoria Street which became the General Post Office's first telephone exchange in 1902.

An extravagant prince and an ambitious architect
The measure of the Royal Mile

In 1811 the lease expired on a dairy farm in Marylebone Park and the land reverted to the Crown. The task of redeveloping it was given to John Nash (1752-1835), the favourite architect of the Prince Regent (later George IV) who at that time was reigning in place of his father George III who was stricken by the blood disorder porphyria. Nash, whose plans were as extravagant as those of the Prince himself, proposed to construct a Royal Mile, beginning in the dairy farm which was to be renamed Regent's Park. It would then run south along Portland Place which took its name from the previous owner of the land, the Duke of Portland. Portland Place owes its generous width to the fact that Lord Foley, the owner of Foley House at its south end (the present site of the Langham Hotel), had a guarantee that no building would ever obscure his view of Hampstead Heath to the north. Portland Place linked with Regent Street and passed to St James's Park via the new Piccadilly Circus and Carlton House Terrace, the home of the Prince. Regent Street itself divides Mayfair, with its aristocratic residences on its west side from Soho, with its immigrant communities, to the east. Needless to say, when buildings had to be demolished to make way for the new road, it was the immigrants who lost out! The lower part of Regent Street where it curves towards Piccadilly Circus, known as the Quadrant, was arcaded, with one of London's first parades of shops at street level and flats above. It was designed in this way so that, in Nash's words, 'Those who have nothing to do all day but walk about and amuse themselves may do so every day in the week instead of being frequently confined to their houses by rain.' Were these the very first 'ladies who lunched'? The shopkeepers complained that the arcade kept out the light and in 1848 they were demolished.

The Royal Mile at Regents Street

SOHO'S IMMIGRANT COMMUNITIES

In the 1670s Soho, which was being turned from a royal hunting park to a cheap residential area, became the home of Greek Christians seeking refuge from Turkish rule. Shortly afterwards French Huguenots settled there, having fled from the persecutions of Louis XIV, and Soho Square still has its Huguenot church. Later residents included Italians and a large Jewish community from Germany and Eastern Europe, one of the most notable being Karl Marx who lived in Dean Street while writing **Das Kapital.** *Soho remains one of London's most lively, tolerant and cosmopolitan communities with a wide range of creative industries.*

Trafalgar Square was created as part of Nash's design, the area having previously been occupied by the Royal Mews. Nash intended that the space be occupied by learned societies like the Royal Society and the Royal Academy but his design was abandoned in favour of one by Charles Barry, architect of the new Palace of Westminster. It was originally to be called William IV Square in honour of one of our less distinguished monarchs but the name Trafalgar Square was adopted on the suggestion of the long-forgotten architect to the Royal Navy George Taylor (1788-1873).

RODS, POLES, PERCHES... BUT NOT AN ANGLER IN SIGHT

On the northern side of the square, in front of the National Gallery, Charles Barry built a terrace on the wall of which in 1876 was engraved a notice which reads:

> *'Imperial Standards of length placed on this site by the Standards Department of the Board of Trade, by Permission of the Commissioners of Her Majesty's Public Buildings and Works: MDCCCLXXVI*

Metal plates set into the wall have the standard lengths of an inch, a foot, two feet and a yard. Along the bottom of the wall is the standard measure of a chain (22 yards) and a standard rod, pole or perch, each of these being one fortieth of a furlong (220 yards). Since the metal plaques expand or contract with varying temperature the standard lengths apply at 62 degrees Fahrenheit.

Nash and pagoda ash

Nash's designs were both costly and controversial. All Soul's, Langham Place, which is at the junction of Portland Place and Regent Street, just in front of the BBC's Broadcasting House, was criticised for its combination of Gothic spire and Classical rotunda. One MP offered to contribute to the cost of pulling it down but it is now cherished as a London landmark. Carlton House, at the bottom of Regent Street overlooking the Mall, was extended as a residence for the Prince Regent and promptly abandoned by him in favour of Buckingham Palace when he became King in 1820. Carlton House was then demolished and its columns used at the front of the National Gallery in Trafalgar Square, where they remain. Nash turned St James's Park from a swamp into the present charming green space, celebrating its opening by a firework display that set fire to the bridge across the lake and a decorative Chinese Pagoda which has since vanished from London's landscape for ever.

ULTIMATE DES RES: THE KING'S HOUSE, PIMLICO

In 1762 George III bought a charming country house on the edge of the built-up area for his mother. It had belonged to the Dukes of Buckingham and became known as 'The King's house, Pimlico,' but today we know it as Buckingham Palace. By the time that John Nash had spent £600,000 (approximately £50m in today's money) on it under the confusing guidance of George IV it had become an uninhabitable wreck. Thomas Cubitt (1788-1855) later turned it into a suitable home for Queen Victoria and her family.

QUEEN VICTORIA'S FAVOURITE BUILDER

Thomas Cubitt was a ship's carpenter who invested his profits from a trading voyage to India to create what became one of the largest construction businesses in England. Besides Belgravia he built much of

Thomas Cubitt

Bloomsbury, Pimlico and Highbury, turning unstable, marshy land into fashionable residential areas. He also rebuilt Buckingham Palace from the wreck left by George IV and John Nash and built Osborne House on the Isle of Wight for Queen Victoria and her family. On his death Victoria wrote that 'a better, kindhearted or more simple, unassuming man never breathed'. He left the longest will ever recorded, at 386 pages; some of his fortune passed to the present Duchess of Cornwall, his direct descendant.

Keeping it in the family
How the posh streets got their names

Many London streets took their names from the people who built them or the families which owned them. Thus the Bloomsbury area of London has many names which reflect the fact that this area, near the British Museum, was originally owned by the Dukes of Bedford (Bedford Square) whose family name is Russell (Russell Square and Great Russell Street); whose home is Woburn Abbey (Woburn Square and Woburn Walk); and whose eldest son is the Marquis of Tavistock (Tavistock Square). The name 'Bloomsbury' itself refers to the manor, or 'bury' of Blemond, William Blemond having bought it in the 13th century. Street names in Mayfair and Belgravia like Grosvenor Square remind us that in the 1720s the area was developed by Sir Richard Grosvenor. In 1677 his father had wisely married the heiress Mary Davies (hence Davies Street) who had inherited much of what is now Mayfair. In the 19th century Thomas Cubitt drained the swamps south of Hyde Park to create Belgrave Square (named after a Grosvenor family property in Leicestershire), Eaton Square (the family home in Cheshire) and Lupus Street (Lupus Grosvenor, 1st Duke of Westminster, 1825-99).

MAYFAIR
Mayfair, bounded by Oxford Street, Regent Street, Piccadilly and Park Lane, takes its name from the fair which was held annually from 1st to 15th May. In 1686 the fair moved from the Haymarket and continued until it was suppressed for rowdyism in 1764. At its heart was Shepherd Market, named after the architect and builder Edward Shepherd. It housed the famous Tiddy Dol's restaurant, specialising in English food and named after the gingerbread maker Tiddy Dol who plied his trade at executions at Tyburn. The restaurant closed while the site was redeveloped.

The history behind the geography
Walking through London's heritage

Other street and district names have earlier origins. Aldwych is one of the most ancient names in London. It is an Anglo-Saxon name which means 'Old settlement' and reflects the fact that it was a trading post outside the walls of the City itself on the way to the separate community to the west of the City which became known as Westminster. King Alfred granted Aldwych, with its valuable trading post, to the Danes as part of the settlement that ended his wars with them. Many places owe their names to royal connections. The King's Road in Chelsea was so called because it was originally a private road which Charles II used to drive to Hampton Court and until 1830 it could be used only on production of a copper pass inscribed 'The King's Private Road'. Pall Mall was laid out in 1661 so that King Charles II could play a game imported originally from Italy called Pallo a Maglio (Ball to Mallet, rather like croquet), close

St James's Palace

to St James's Palace. The road was officially called Catherine Street, after Charles's Queen Catherine of Braganza but soon took on the name of the game for which it was designed. South of the Strand are a number of streets whose names between them spell out the name of the Stuart courtier and landowner the 2nd Duke of Buckingham, 'George Villiers of Buckingham'. These are George Court; Villiers Street; Of Alley (since renamed York Place); and Buckingham Street.

Soho was from 1536 a royal hunting park for Whitehall Palace, 'So-ho!' being a contemporary hunting cry. Smoothfield which lay just outside the City boundary became Smithfield, a place of execution before it became a live cattle market noted for its disorderly character. In 1866 the present meat market was designed by Horace Jones, the architect also of Tower Bridge.

WHITEHALL PALACE

This magnificent Tudor palace was created by Henry VIII after he took over the site from Cardinal Wolsey when the latter fell from favour. It may have owed its name to the light stone from which it was built. In 1698 it was burned to the ground, only the Banqueting House surviving. The palace's name survives in the street in which it was situated and has thereby given its name to the activities of government in general, as in 'Whitehall has decreed that...' The authoritarian Henry VIII would surely have approved!

Hug a Huguenot

Other names have more obscure origins. Bedlam, a synonym for an asylum, took its name from the Priory of St Mary Bethlehem in Bishopsgate, founded in 1247 and later used for accommodating the mentally ill. In 1815 the hospital was moved to Lambeth where its premises were later occupied by the Imperial War Museum. The nearby Elephant

and Castle probably owes its name to the Infanta of Castile (the eldest daughter of the then King of Spain) who was at one time engaged to Charles I. Spitalfields also has foreign associations, having become the home of immigrant Huguenot silk weavers in the late 17th century. The word spital is a shortened form of 'hospital' and the area takes its name from the St Mary Spital, a hospital founded in the 12th century. Finsbury to the north of central London owes its name to the fact that it was once part of the Great Fen, a marshy area which lay just outside the City walls.

In 1849 the humorous magazine *Punch* suggested some street names which reflected the insanitary state of the capital in the pre-Bazalgette years. *Punch* suggested Open Sewer Street; Slaughter House Buildings; Shambles Place; Knacker's Yard; Graveyard Crescent; Charnel Square; Typhus Alley; Scrofula Lane; Consumption Alley, and so on.

A well-appointed city
London's watery resources

Many London placenames have their origins in water supplies. Marylebone is an abbreviation for Mary-le-bourne, the word 'bourne' meaning a spring. Its water was conducted in a lead pipe to the Great Conduit at Cheapside in the City in 1236 from which citizens could draw water free of charge. Conduit Street, off Regent Street, and Lamb's Conduit Passage in Holborn were also the location of water conduits. Holywell, near Liverpool Street Station, Clement's Well near the Monument and Clerkenwell all mark the sites of former wells as

The Great Conduit

does Sadler's Wells. The last of these became a fashionable spa in the 18th century and the original well may still be glimpsed through a glass floor panel behind the scenes at Sadler's Wells theatre. New River Head, next to Sadler's Wells in Rosebery Avenue, marked the terminus of the New River Company. The brainchild of Hugh Myddleton, Welsh silversmith and City entrepreneur, the New River was built between 1609 and 1613 to bring water by gravity from the Chiltern Hills near Ware to the city. It now stops short at Stoke Newington where it feeds into the London Ring Main and continues to supply Londoners with water four centuries after its construction. In the abandoned stretch beyond Stoke Newington it survives in small lakes and the original waterworks and cistern may be seen off Rosebery Avenue. Cold Bath Square in Clerkenwell marks the site of a facility which flourished until 1878 and is now close to the home of the Royal Mail's main sorting office at Mount Pleasant. Teddington, west of London, was originally called 'Tide-end-Town', a reference to the fact that it is the place where the Thames ceases to be a tidal river, now marked by Teddington Lock.

Property magnates with stiff collars
The grounds for the invention of retail therapy

Many of London's most elegant shopping streets were designed for residential purposes and did not acquire a significant number of shops until the 19th century. In the early 17th century a tailor called Robert Baker made a fortune from selling a stiff collar of his own design known as a picadil. In 1612 he built himself a fine mansion in Great Windmill Street, close to the present junction of Piccadilly Circus and Shaftesbury Avenue. Envious aristocrats who resented the wealth of this arriviste dubbed his new home Piccadilly in reference to the source of his wealth and the name became associated with the road on land that Baker also owned. Later in the century the nearby Jermyn Street drew its name from Henry Jermyn, Earl of St Albans who received the land by

a grant of Charles II whose exile he had shared during Oliver Cromwell's Protectorate. A building on the corner of Jermyn Street and Bury Street has a relief, dating from about 1680, showing the king presenting the deeds to Jermyn. Four years later a property developer called Thomas Bond began to develop Bond Street as a smart residential quarter which accommodated such 'celebrities' as Jonathan Swift, Edward Gibbon and Horatio Nelson.

The first purpose-built shopping precinct was Burlington Arcade, opened in 1819 for Lord George Cavendish. Its smart, uniformed beadles in their top hats and capes are in effect a private constabulary and pre-date the Metropolitan Police by ten years. Rather like school monitors they are responsible for maintaining good behaviour amongst those who walk through the arcade and particularly for ensuring that there is no whistling, singing, running or carrying of opened umbrellas.

EROTIC REVIEW?
Piccadilly Circus was created in 1819 to form an elegant junction between

The Statue of Anteros

Regent Street, Piccadilly and the later Shaftesbury Avenue. It had to wait until 1893 for the statue of Anteros to be unveiled. Yes, that's right – the statue is that of Anteros, the Greek god of unselfish love, to commemorate the work of the 7th Earl of Shaftesbury who had devoted his life to campaigning on behalf of the poor, especially children. It was unveiled in 1893 and soon became mistaken for Eros, the god of romantic love – which would probably not have pleased the puritanical earl. It was the first statue in the world to be cast in aluminium.

The large retail shops which now dominate the area appeared from the latter half of the 19th century, the major exception being Fortnum and Mason which opened as a grocery store in the 1770s close to its present site. It was founded by Charles Fortnum, a footman in the household of George III who used his knowledge of the needs of the royal household, and his friend John Mason, a groom, who organised the deliveries.

Savile Row's first tailors arrived in its smart residences from the 1850s. In 1875 Arthur Liberty opened a shop in Regent Street, calling it East India House, and specialised in selling fine silks. In 1881 the shop became very popular when librettist WS Gilbert and composer Arthur Sullivan incorporated Liberty fabrics in costumes for their comic operetta *Patience*; its designs also became associated with the work of the Pre-Raphaelites and William Morris. The sports shop Lillywhites began to trade near Euston Station in 1863, the enterprise of a family of cricketers. It did not move to Piccadilly Circus until 1925 where it remains, still the nation's largest sports store beloning to Sports Direct. In 1909 the flamboyant American Gordon Selfridge opened London's largest department store on Oxford Street on a site which in 1765 had been occupied by a furniture store bearing the name of the Waring family (later Waring and Gillow). In the meantime Waring and Gillow had moved to new premises in Oxford Street. Sam Waring encouraged Selfridge's new enterprise on condition that Selfridge did not sell furniture, a promise he kept. The Waring and Gillow stores closed in the 1980s but Selfridges continues to thrive.

THE LONDON PANTHEON

In 1772 the architect James Wyatt opened the Pantheon (Greek, 'to every god') on Oxford Street as a place of entertainment with card rooms, tea rooms and music rooms. Its design was based on that of the Hagia Sophia in Constantinople (now Istanbul). It became in turn an exhibition centre, theatre, opera house and bazaar, each of them being financially unrewarding. In 1937 the site at last became

profitable when it was bought by retailer Marks and Spencer who kept the name Pantheon for the store.

Shops defunct – and Harrods

Some once well-known names have not survived. Jackson's of Piccadilly was established as a wax and tallow chandler by the 1820s though it later became established as a food shop, famous for its teas. Its name survives on branded goods supplied to other retailers but the shop closed in 1980. The same is true of the men's outfitters Simpson's of Piccadilly which closed in 1999 and became bookseller Waterstone's largest store. The TV scriptwriter Jeremy Lloyd worked at Simpson's as a young man and drew on his experiences when writing the popular television comedy *Are You Being Served?* A name now forgotten is that of James Shoolbred, a large department store on Tottenham Court Road which specialised in fine furniture, much of it made in-house, and other wooden artefacts, notably jigsaw puzzles. It traded from the 1820s and closed in 1931. Gamages traded from premises in High Holborn from 1878 to 1972.

It was created by Arthur Gamage, a farmer's son from Herefordshire who bought up a number of ill-assorted properties which were not designed to be used together, making a trip to Gamages an exercise in direction-finding as well as retail therapy. It was strong on toys, sports and camping equipment (being official supplier to the Scout Association) and a pioneer in the use of mail order catalogues. Its location – like that of Shoolbred's rather remote from the traditional shopping district of the West End – proved an insuperable problem and it closed in 1972 to make way for offices. Only Harrods has managed to thrive as a major department store independent of the West End. In 1849, in the distant village of Knightsbridge, Henry Harrod, a tea merchant, bought a small grocer's which benefited from the proximity of the Great Exhibition of 1851, many visitors flocking to his store with its motto of Omnia Omnibus Ubique ('all things for everyone, everywhere'). By 1867 the store had the astonishing turnover of almost £1,000 a week. Its turnover now approaches £1 billion a year.

Royal rowing and dodgy dealing
The story of Leicester Square

Leicester Square, in the heart of London's theatre district, has at its centre a statue of William Shakespeare, beneath which is an inscription explaining that the square was presented to the citizens of London by Albert Grant. It doesn't tell the reader where the money came from. The district took its name from Leicester House, built in 1636 as the London home of the Earls of Leicester. In the 18th century it became the home first of the future George II and later of his son Frederick, Prince of Wales, each in turn using it as a base to pursue the Hanoverian tradition of sons quarrelling with fathers. In 1806 Leicester House was demolished and

Leicester Square

the square became a derelict eyesore: an equestrian statue of George I was vandalised by early graffiti artists, the rider being supplied with a broom in place of a sword and the horse covered in spots. Attempts to revive the square's fortunes with such entertainments as 'Mr Wylde's Great Globe' failed as these descended into bankruptcy.

In 1873 Albert Grant – who styled himself 'Baron' after an honour supposedly granted to him by the new Kingdom of Italy – offered to buy the square and refurbish it at his own expense. He neglected to mention that he had gained his money as an early exponent of the black art of direct mailing, enticing widows and clergyman to invest in such non-existent enterprises as the Emma Silver Mine and the Labuan Coal Company. He raised £24 million from such hopeful investors, of which £20 million was never seen again. From such sources he paid for the square to be cleared, landscaped and supplied with statues of Isaac Newton, Joshua Reynolds, William Hogarth and the surgeon William Hunter, who had all lived in the area. A statue of Charlie Chaplin has since been added. Grant – whose birth name was Albert Gottheimer – built a magnificent house near Kensington Palace which was seized by his creditors, the staircase being bought by Madame Tussaud's where it remains. He died in penury in 1899, his obituary in the *Illustrated London News* recording that he was 'a man of agreeable presence and enthusiastic manners whose death brought back to mind many an ancient adventure of his as promoter, mineowner, millionaire and bankrupt'.

Secure foundations
London's inspirational institutions

Some of London's most amazing institutions have disappeared but are remembered by street names and similar mementoes. One of the strangest is St Martin's-le-Grand. Founded as a monastery and college by two brothers in the reign of Edward the Confessor, its bells sounded the nightly curfew until this role was taken over by those of St-Mary-le-Bow in the 14th century. Criminals could seek sanctuary

St Martin's-le-Grand

within its grounds until 1697 when this privilege was ended. Sir Thomas More claimed that Miles Forrest, one of those accused of the murder of the Princes in the Tower, 'rotted away piecemeal' in the sanctuary. The foundation was dissolved by Henry VIII in the 1540s and became noted for its production of jewellery and fine lace. It became the site of the headquarters of the Post Office in 1829.

Nearby are the sites of two famous schools. Christ's Hospital was founded in Newgate Street by Edward VI in 1553, shortly before his death, as a hospital for orphans in the buildings formerly occupied by the Greyfriars monastery before it was dissolved. It is known as the Blue Coat School because of its distinctive uniform. In 1666 most of the buildings were destroyed in the Great Fire and it was rebuilt to designs by Christopher Wren and Nicholas Hawksmoor. Past pupils have included the poets Coleridge and Lamb and the Catholic martyr Edmund Campion. The school moved to Horsham, Sussex, in 1902 and the London site was taken over, like that of St Martin's-le-Grand, by the Post Office. Just to the north the Charterhouse is remembered by the street which bears its name. Bought in 1348 as a burial ground for victims of the Black Death, it soon became a Carthusian monastery, accommodating a particularly ascetic order of monks who could talk to one another only on Sundays after a meal when they were permitted a 3 hour walk outside the monastery walls. The monks declined to recognise Henry VIII as head of the

Charterhouse School

church and most were executed. In 1611, Thomas Sutton (1532-1611), reputedly 'the richest commoner in England' as a result of his ownership of coal mines in Northumberland, acquired the property and founded Charterhouse School whose pupils are known as Carthusians. He also founded the adjacent hospital for 80 'Poore Brethren'. The school moved to Godalming, Surrey in 1872 and the buildings, restored after being bombed in 1941, now accommodate St Bartholomew's Hospital Medical School. It also provides a home for 40 Charterhouse Pensioners known as

Brothers who have to have been born in London. One of the better known recent brothers is the novelist Simon Raven.

Cannon from steel

Steelyard Passage on the banks of the Thames near Cannon Street Station marks the former site of the London base of the Hanseatic League, a trading confederation of north European cities stretching from Novgorod in Russia to Bruges in Belgium. The Steelyard, which took its name from scales used to weigh imports and exports, was in effect a warehouse and its merchants enjoyed many privileges, including a monopoly of wool exports, in return for which they paid taxes to the monarch, most notably to Edward III to finance the Hundred Years' War against France. Elizabeth I abolished these privileges in 1598 and the Steelyard continued to be used as a warehouse and also as a Rhenish Garden where wines from Germany as well as beer could be enjoyed in open air comfort. Samuel Pepys makes several references to his use of its facilities in his diary. The

Steelyard was finally sold in 1853 for the handsome sum of £72,500 to become the site of Cannon Street Station. A plaque was unveiled in 2005 at Cannon Street Station to mark the former site of the Steelyard.

Water, water, everywhere
London's 'lost' rivers

For many people the essence of London is the River Thames but very few realise that the city's major waterway is fed by tributaries which still flow among or beneath the streets of the capital. Some of them occasionally emerge in the form of lakes while others pass through very unlikely places. The most extraordinary is the River Westbourne. Like most of the rivers north of the river it rises on Hampstead Heath. It then flows, mostly beneath the streets, surfacing in Hyde Park as the Serpentine and then passing through a conduit above the trains at Sloane Square Underground Station where the large and odd-shaped metal tube puzzles observant waiting passengers.

The Tyburn, which also begins on Hampstead Heath, appears as the pond in Regent's Park and passes beneath Marble Arch where it gave its name to the site of public executions, in use until 1783. It then passes beneath Buckingham Palace before forming a delta and entering the Thames in two branches, one at Millbank and the other near Westminster Underground Station. Enterprising Victorians used to make subterranean voyages along these rivers. In 1862 one of them, John Hollingshead, rowed with some friends along the Tyburn until he estimated they were beneath Buckingham Palace, at which point they all stood, removed their hats and sang 'God save the Queen'! The third major river to the north, the Fleet, has two sources, in Hampstead and Highgate ponds, and flows beneath the streets between King's Cross and St Pancras Stations before passing through Clerkenwell underneath the Farringdon Road and entering the Thames just upstream from Blackfriars Station. At low tide its outlet into the Thames is clearly visible from the platforms stretching over the river. It was at one time a substantial river, navigable as far as Old Bourne (Holborn). In the reign of Edward II the Fleet was large enough to harbour pirates who emerged from it to attack the king's barge as it passed up the Thames. The unseen river has, of course, given its name to Fleet Street nearby. The last of the major rivers to the north is the River Lea (also spelt Lee) which rises at Leagrave, near Luton in the Chilterns, and flows mostly above ground. It is most often seen in the opening credits of *EastEnders* as it enters the Thames opposite the Millennium Dome. Other rivers to the north include Stamford Brook in Acton; Counter's Creek which flows beneath Chelsea's football ground at Stamford Bridge; and the Walbrook which gives its name to a street and a church behind the Mansion House in the heart of the City.

SAMARITAN SANCTUARY

This charming little church is one of Christopher Wren's finest, and gives its name to the street and to St Stephen's, Walbrook, behind the Mansion House. It has a beautiful dome supported by twelve columns, and lots of natural light despite surrounding buildings. It is the home of the Samaritans, founded in 1953 by the rector of St Stephen, Reverend Chad Varah (1911-2007), to talk to the suicidal and despairing.

The river system to the south is equally diverse and these rivers are more likely to be seen above ground. Beverley Brook rises at Worcester Park and may be seen crossing Wimbledon Common, entering the Thames near Putney Bridge. The River Wandle draws on rainfall from the North Downs in its two sources, one near Croydon and the other at Carshalton Ponds and is mostly above ground, notably in Wandsworth. The main source of the Effra is near Crystal Palace from where it flows mostly underground to Vauxhall. The Ravensbourne rises at Caesar's Well, Keston, close to a Roman camp south of Bromley and flows mostly above ground to join the Thames at Deptford Creek where Francis Drake was knighted by Elizabeth I in 1580. Drake had moored his ship the *Golden Hind* in the creek and the vessel, much battered after its three year circumnavigation of the world, remained there until it was broken up and its timbers put to other uses, including the building of a cupboard for the Middle Temple.

Other rivers to the south include the Falconbrook which runs underground from Tooting Bec common to Battersea; and the Peck, Earl's Sluice and Neckringer which rise in East Dulwich and enter the Thames between Bermondsey and Rotherhithe.

During the Middle Ages these rivers were used to supply water for drinking and washing and the *Domesday Book*, dating from 1086, recorded many watermills as a source of power. By 1800 the expansion and urbanisation of London had ensured that most of them were covered over. After 1815 they became the means by which much of London's sewage was conveyed to the Thames, sometimes with unforeseen consequences. In 1846 the foetid gases in the River Fleet caused an explosion, despatching a tide of sewage through the streets which swept away three houses in Clerkenwell.

'Neath the Shade of the Ruislip Poplars
The joys of Metro-land

Metro-land, and the style of suburban living which it represented, is associated with the poet John Betjeman but the name and the place were created by the Metropolitan Railway. The railway's managers soon realised that long-distance commuters would generate more revenue than could be earned from journeys within London, not to mention the substantial profits that would arise from property development. In 1915 the railway published a booklet called *Metro-land* which encouraged its passengers to purchase homes built on land owned by the railway and adjacent to its tracks. Half of its pages were devoted to advertisements by builders which enabled the booklet to be sold for two old pence (less than 1p). All the arts of estate agency marketing were brought to bear including a song called ''Neath the Shade of the Ruislip Poplars' which ended with the excruciating:

'It's a very short distance by rail on

the Met
And at the gate you'll find waiting,
sweet Violet.'

Neither this nor the accompanying 'Poplars Waltz' made a lasting mark on British culture but they sold houses. Neasden was described as 'A Model Garden Village. Peace and quiet prevail and the stretches of country around offer plenty of opportunity for invigorating exercise.'

SACRE BLEU, LA TOUR DE NEASDEN? NON, MERCI!

The most bizarre example of property development was the brainchild of Sir Edward Watkin (1819-1901), chairman of the Metropolitan Railway. Based upon the Eiffel Tower but 15 feet higher, Watkin's Folly was intended to generate millions of fare-paying passengers for the Metropolitan Railway. Neasden did not prove to be as attractive as Paris and the structure never grew above the first level. It was demolished in 1907 to make way for Wembley Stadium.

Other Underground railways soon followed suit. The Northern Line developed Edgware which was described in 1926 as 'a beautiful garden suburb, on a hillside facing south, protected from north winds and catching every gleam of sunshine'. Prices were competitive in all these developments. A four-bedroom detached house in Rickmansworth could be bought for £1,400, with a deposit of £150!

The most luxurious accommodation of all was at Baker Street Station, headquarters of the Metropolitan Railway. It was called Chiltern Court and consisted of half a million square feet of shops and luxury flats built above the station. Harrods declined the opportunity to open a branch there but flats, ranging from ten-room Mansion flats to three-room Bachelor flats, were in heavy demand. The first occupants included the writers Arnold Bennett and HG Wells.

Hampstead to New Delhi

One of the more unusual suburban developments was Hampstead Garden Suburb which resulted from a determined campaign by Henrietta Barnett to prevent inappropriate development close to Hampstead Heath by the Charing Cross, Euston and Hampstead Railway (later part of the Northern Line). She raised over £200,000 from sympathetic supporters to build residences 'where different social classes could live together in harmony'. Much of it was designed by distinguished architects such as Sir Edwin Lutyens who was also the architect of New Delhi. It remains a community where development is strictly controlled to ensure the maintenance of the architects' harmonious environment.

TOYNBEE HALL

Henrietta Barnett and her husband the Reverend Samuel Barnett founded Toynbee Hall in Samuel's parish of Whitechapel in 1884 to provide educational and social facilities for the poor of London's East End. It continues to thrive on its original site in Commercial Street where in its early days it attracted the admiration of the young Clement Attlee and set him on the path which led him to Downing Street in 1945.

What lies beneath
London's hidden tube stations

Several Underground stations are no longer in use but one station rests undisturbed beneath Hampstead Heath, having never opened. This is North End Station on the Northern Line between Hampstead and Golders Green. The station was built by Charles Yerkes, chairman of the Charing Cross, Euston and Hampstead Railway in anticipation of a steady flow of commuters but Henrietta Barnett's successful campaign to protect Hampstead

Charles Tyson Yerkes

Heath from development ensured that the station, though completed, never opened. On 29th September 1940, at the height of the Battle of Britain, it was used for a Cabinet meeting since it was, in Churchill's words 'far from the light of day'. Above the station is a small white building which appears to be an electrical sub-station but is in fact an entrance to the platforms. A Home Guard sentry was standing by its door on the day of the meeting, 'when Mr Churchill popped out of the ground at my feet'. The disused Down Street station, between Hyde Park Corner and Green Park on the Piccadilly Line was also used for Cabinet meetings.

ANY OLD IRON

Charles Tyson Yerkes (1837-1905) was a colourful entrepreneur from Philadelphia where he was briefly gaoled for fraud and who later fled from Chicago when investors in his transit system lost nearly all their money. He arrived in London in 1901 and by a series of strange manoeuvres raised money to buy or build most of the Underground railway network, leaving it on the verge of bankruptcy.

His oft-repeated motto was 'Buy up old junk, fix it up a little and unload it upon other fellows.' Most of his investors were from the Continent and America since the City distrusted him. Perhaps they were wiser in those days!

The oldest disused station is King William Street Station, just north of London Bridge. It was opened in 1890 as the terminus of the City and South London Railway and closed within ten years when London Bridge Station opened. A proposal to use it for growing mushrooms was not pursued and it came back into the news in 1914 when some excitable newspapers suggested that it harboured a nest of enemy agents. A search by the City police yielded no results. In January 1940 it was equipped as an air raid shelter and it is now used, as are many other disused stations, as an archive store by the tenants of the modern office building, Regis House, which sits above it.

Ghost train

The lost station to which most myths cling is that of South Kentish

Town, between Camden Town and Kentish Town, on the Northern Line. It closed in 1924 and became the subject of a persistent story that a passenger had alighted there and remained marooned until he caught the eye of a passing driver several days later. John Betjeman encouraged the tale in a radio broadcast of 1951. The station's booking hall remains a conspicuous feature of Kentish Town Road. British Museum Station, situated between Tottenham Court Road and Chancery Lane, closed in 1933 when Holborn Station was enlarged; a newspaper offered a reward to anyone who would spend a night at the disused station to look for the rumoured ancient Egyptian ghost which supposedly occupied it. The reward was never claimed.

The Marylebone Cricket Club (MCC) had its own station, Lord's, on the Metropolitan and St John's Wood Railway for a few months in 1939 but when the Bakerloo Line opened to Stanmore in November of that year with its own St John's Wood Station (now on the Jubilee Line) Lord's closed 'temporarily' but was never to reopen. However, one underground station survives with sporting connotations. In 1932 Herbert Chapman, the legendary manager of Arsenal FC, persuaded the Piccadilly Line to change the name of its Gillespie Road Station to Arsenal, which it remains.

Capital crime and punishment
London's famous prisons

London is home to more prisons than any other city. The most notorious have closed but they are remembered in street names and bits of them are to be found in unlikely places including a famous art gallery. There were five separate prisons at Newgate during its long history. The first was the gatehouse in London's Roman Wall through which travellers were admitted to the City itself. Its

Millbank Prison

use as a prison dates from the 12th century. In the 15th century the prison had fallen into such disrepair that the Mayor of London, Richard Whittington, left money in his will for it to be rebuilt. In 1628, faced with the enduring problem of prison overcrowding, an 'early release' scheme was instituted by Charles I whereby prisoners could be freed provided that they enlisted in the army or navy. Whittington's prison, which featured a statue of the mayor accompanied by a cat, survived until it was destroyed by the Great Fire of 1666 and by the 1770s its successor, the third prison, was itself in a poor state of repair. A fourth Newgate was therefore built but enjoyed a very brief existence since it was destroyed in the Gordon Riots of 1780. The fifth and final Newgate, which arose from the ashes of the fourth, survived until 1902 when it was demolished to make way for an enlarged Old Bailey. Some of its walls may still be seen behind the Old Bailey itself.

MEN OF STRAW
In the 18th century, trials at the Old Bailey, which was conveniently situated next to Newgate prison, lasted on average 11 minutes. This inordinately speedy process was helped by the availability of so-called witnesses who loitered outside the court with bits of straw protruding from their pockets or shoes as a signal that they were prepared to give evidence for whichever side was willing to pay them: hence the expression 'men of straw'.

Other prisons which have now vanished also have their claims to fame. The Fleet Prison was situated on the banks of the River Fleet, close to the place where Fleet Street meets Ludgate Circus. Its inmates included the poet John Donne and the Quaker William Penn, founder of Pennsylvania. Samuel Pickwick was sent to the Fleet Prison by Dickens for allegedly failing to honour a pledge of marriage and Falstaff was despatched there for numerous offences, to his great indignation, at the end of Shakespeare's *King Henry IV, Part II.* Dickens's father was imprisoned in the Marshalsea Prison for debt as was Marc Brunel, father of Isambard. The prison was closed in 1842, one wall remaining in Angel Place just off Borough High Street in Southwark where a commemorative plaque reminds visitors of its history. Nearby, in Clink Street, is a museum marking the site of the Bishop of Winchester's Prison, the Clink, (giving us the expression 'in the Clink') which was for citizens who broke the peace on Bankside. It was burned down in the Gordon Riots of 1780 and never rebuilt.

TEARING DOWN THE WALLS

The Gordon Riots occurred in June of 1780 and were led by a deranged Scottish aristocrat called Lord George Gordon. They were a protest against some proposals to relax restrictions on Roman Catholics which had been introduced under Elizabeth I. Five days of mayhem, initially directed against Catholic sympathisers and chapels, led to widespread destruction, Newgate Prison being one of many casualties. Twenty-one were hanged, Gordon himself being spared on the grounds that his intentions were peaceful though he was later gaoled in the rebuilt Newgate in 1788 for insulting Marie Antoinette, and died there. The riots are commemorated in Charles Dickens's novel **Barnaby Rudge: a Tale of the Riots of Eighty.**

Modern art cells

Millbank Prison opened in 1821 with a capacity of over 1,000 inmates and became known as 'The Fattening House' because of its generous diet which was swiftly made less attractive following a press campaign. Its swampy site led to many deaths amongst prisoners and for this reason it was closed in 1890 to make way for the Tate Gallery (now Tate Britain) which incorporates some of Millbank's materials in its fabric.

The largest of London's gaols was at Coldbath Fields with a capacity of 1,200 inmates. It was demolished in 1889 to make way for the Royal Mail's Mount Pleasant sorting office. Its regime was notoriously harsh and was celebrated in verse by Coleridge:

As he went through Coldbath Fields he saw
A solitary cell,
And the Devil was pleased, for it gave him a hint

For improving his prisons in Hell.

Both Millbank and Coldbath Fields adopted the 'Silent and Solitary' systems of imprisonment whereby prisoners were denied all contact with other inmates in the belief that they would thereby reflect on the error of their ways. Many went mad.

Newgate procession

MAKE LIKE A HAMSTER, OR ELSE!

Besides recommending isolation Victorian penal reformers believed in keeping prisoners occupied. Unpicking oakum (dense knots of tarred rope) was bad enough but the punishment most dreaded was the treadwheel which required a prisoner to ascend the equivalent of 12,000 feet on a diet of bread and gruel. To avoid it prisoners would swallow soap to bring on a fever accompanied by foaming at the mouth. The treadwheel was abolished in 1898.

The journey to the scaffold
Newgate's morbid processions

Those who were found guilty at the Old Bailey were often sentenced to death since in the 18th century over 300 offences carried the death penalty, including theft of goods worth more than five shillings and impersonating a Chelsea Pensioner. On the evening before the executions a sermon would be preached in the chapel at Newgate in the presence of the condemned, a coffin being prominently placed in the centre of the chapel to remind the prisoners of the fate which awaited them. Gaolers, ever anxious to supplement their incomes, admitted to the service curious members of the public who were prepared to pay for the privilege. The sermon would be preached by a clergyman appointed by the bishop called the Newgate 'Ordinary' who profited from the role by publishing accounts of confessions supposedly obtained from prisoners. At midnight the sexton of St Sepulchre's Church opposite the Old Bailey would ring a bell outside the condemned cell and recite a verse beginning, 'All you that in the condemned cell do lie, Repent you, for tomorrow you shall die.'

St Sepulchre's still contains mementoes of its association with Newgate. An 'Ordinary' called Villette prepared for sale a confession by a young condemned boy in the 1770s. Upon being told that another suspect had confessed to the crime and that a reprieve for the boy was on the way, Villette feared a loss on his carefully prepared 'confession' and urged the executioner to proceed, protesting that it was no time to be worrying about 'details of this kind'! The boy was spared by more compassionate authorities.

On the morning of executions the 'Newgate procession' would set out for Tyburn, on the present site of Marble Arch, where the former scaffold is commemorated by a brass plaque. The prisoners would travel in carts along the present route of High Holborn, New Oxford Street and Oxford Street. They were led by the highwaymen who were the acknowledged aristocrats of the criminal fraternity, followed by murderers, rapists and thieves, with traitors drawn on hurdles bringing up the rear. The streets would be lined with spectators, often drunk, shouting encouragement or abuse to the occupants of the carts, throwing missiles and offering to buy drinks for them. The procession would indeed stop at numerous taverns on the route so that, with luck, the prisoners would themselves often be drunk before they reached Tyburn. This was fortunate since, until the introduction of the 'Newgate Drop' in 1760 which brought about instant death by breaking the neck, most prisoners died by strangulation, often taking 15 or 20 minutes to do so and urinating in the process; or, as the spectators called it, 'pissing when you can't whistle'. And the spectators were numerous. An enterprising lady erected stands called 'Mother Proctor's Pews', charging as much as £10, a huge sum in the 18th century, for seats with the best view.

Once merciful death had arrived there would be a stampede towards the corpses, amongst which three rival groups could usually be discerned. First there were those suffering from warts who believed that the 'death sweat' of the prisoners would relieve this condition. They sought to collect the perspiration from the skins of the corpses. Secondly there were the beadles of the College of Surgeons and the London teaching hospitals who wanted the corpses for dissection. Finally there were the friends and relatives of the executed who wanted to spare them these and other such indignities. Fisticuffs were commonplace.

No hanging around

In 1783 executions were moved from Tyburn to a scaffold outside Newgate (now the site of the Old Bailey) because of public concern about the disorder arising from the Newgate processions. Not everyone was pleased. Dr Samuel Johnson complained that, 'Executions are intended to draw spectators. If they do not draw spectators they don't answer their purpose. The old method was most satisfactory to all parties; the public was gratified by a procession; the criminal was supported by it. Why is all this to be swept away?' Charles Dickens and William Thackeray both witnessed executions outside Newgate and found them degrading. Dickens wrote of the 'ribaldry, levity, drunkenness and flaunting vice' of the crowd, the only decorum occurring with the cry of 'Hats off' as the moment of execution arrived. Thackeray, in his celebrated essay 'On Going to see a Man Hanged', wrote 'I have been abetting an act of frightful wickedness and violence.' In 1868, as a result of such criticisms, executions were moved to within the prison walls itself. One thousand, one hundred and six men and 49 women were hanged within Newgate between 1868 and the demolition of the prison in 1902 when the scaffold was moved to Pentonville where it remained in use until 1961, its victims including Dr Hawley Crippen (hanged 1910) and the Irish Nationalist Roger Casement (hanged 1916).

'Yours truly, Jack the Ripper'
The Whitechapel terror writes

The Whitechapel terror

One criminal who did not meet his end at the end of a hangman's noose was the murderer who terrorised Whitechapel between August and November 1888 with five gruesome murders; the culprit has become known as Jack the Ripper. The name arose from a teasing letter sent to the press at the height of the frenzy, signed 'Yours truly, Jack the Ripper'. It is unlikely that the letter was penned by the murderer himself but the name stuck to the mystery perpetrator because of his habit of subjecting his victims to horrific mutilations. The terror lasted longer than the three months of the five murders since other murders were committed in the lawless area of Whitechapel which were doubtfully attributed to 'Jack'; but the so-called canonical five had sufficient similarities in method to be placed with some confidence at his door. A relatively short walk takes in all the murder scenes. Jack the Ripper was not the first London serial killer and certainly neither the last nor the most prolific but he is surely the most notorious.

All the women murdered were prostitutes plying their trade and all the murders occurred within little more than half a mile of one another. Many street names were later changed either because of the demolition of slums or to conceal the notoriety conferred by the Ripper murders. The first was that of Mary Ann Nicholas on 31st August 1888 at Buck's Row, now Durward Street, north of the Whitechapel Road. The next victim, within eight days, was Anne Chapman on 8th September, in a yard behind 29, Hanbury Street, within 300 yards of the first. The murders were linked because of the mutilations inflicted on the victims. Just over three weeks later, on 30th September, Elizabeth

Stride was murdered at 40, Berner Street (now Henriques Street) and the same night Catherine Eddowes met her end at Mitre Square, just within the City boundary about three-quarters of a mile to the west. All these murders were carried out in streets, in some haste. There was then an interval of nearly six weeks before the last and most horrific of the canonical murders. Mary Jane Kelly took her murderer back to her room at Miller's Court behind Dorset Street (later Duval Street) where, in the privacy of her room, he had time to mutilate her to a greater extent than any of the previous victims. Duval Street no longer exists, its site occupied by a multi-storey car park south of Spitalfields Market close to White's Row.

Join the list...

So who was Jack the Ripper? A small and continuing industry has arisen devoted to identifying him, some of the suggestions involving a high level of imagination and the occasional forgery. Many candidates have been put forward, the most fanciful being the Duke of Clarence, eldest son of Edward VII, who died before he could inherit the throne which passed (together with his fiancée Mary of Teck) to his younger brother George V. Other imaginative suggestions have included the artist Walter Sickert, the mild and shy Lewis Carroll (author of Alice's Adventures in Wonderland), and a Liverpool cotton merchant called James Maybrick whose wife was later convicted of poisoning him. The person upon whom fell the suspicions of the police was a Jew of Polish origin called Aaron Kosminski who was later committed to Colney Hatch Lunatic Asylum by his family, the suggestion being that they did this to shield him from the law. He died shortly afterwards and was the suspect named with some confidence by Chief Inspector Donald Swanson (1848-1924) of the Metropolitan Police who supervised the investigation. According to this account Kosminski was not prosecuted because the only witness to the murders, Israel Schwartz, was himself a Jew who would not testify against a fellow Jew. There are serious doubts about this claim.

The long and short arms of the law
London's police forces

Few citizens realise that, as well as Britain's largest police service, London also accommodates the smallest, the City Police. The Metropolitan Police took office in September 1829, created by the Home Secretary Sir Robert Peel whose name was immediately adopted by the public to describe the new constables ('Bobbies' or 'Peelers'). They replaced the old system of local watchmen known as Charlies who had been established during the reign of Charles II and consisted mainly of elderly and feeble men. They gave us the expression 'Proper Charlies', signifying someone ineffective. The new constables were given a uniform (with a top hat) which was deliberately unmilitary in appearance since opponents of the new force feared that it would be used to oppress the population. They were paid three shillings a day, a poor wage even for 1829 and within four years fewer than 500 of the original 3,000 constables were still in the service.

The headquarters of the new force was at 4, Whitehall Place, adjacent to a police station entered from Scotland Yard, a name quickly associated with the new force. In 1842 a detective department was established. In 1830 William IV became King and constables were issued with a wooden wand of office which signified their authority. Around the top of the wand was a copper band engraved W IV R (William IV Rex). William IV was commonly referred to as 'Old Bill' or 'Silly Billy'; the constables became known as Coppers or the Old Bill, names which have stuck.

The Bow Street Runners had been set up in the 1750s by Henry Fielding (author of *Tom Jones*) and his brother John as an alternative to the ineffective Charlies and corrupt thief takers which preceded them. They were based at Bow Street Magistrates' Court, Covent Garden, where the brothers dispensed justice with an honesty formerly absent from their predecessors, the Basket Justices, who openly carried baskets which invited bribes from those attending court.

The Bow Street Runners quickly rid Covent Garden of the gangs of organised criminals who plagued the area and were soon joined by a mounted force which ranged over a wider area. The Bow Street Runners were merged with the Metropolitan Police in 1839, along with the Thames River police. Bow Street remained a magistrates' court until July 2006 when its last case concerned an alcoholic vagrant. Its work was transferred to Westminster Magistrates' Court. Bow Street Court and police station are in the process of being converted into a prison-style (!) hotel. Bow Street police station was the only one to have a white lamp outside rather than the famous standard blue lamp so that Queen Victoria, on her visits to the opera, would not be reminded of the Blue Room at Windsor Castle where Prince Albert had died in 1861, the year blue lamps were introduced.

Jonathan Wild

THE SUPERGRASS

Thief takers earned money by informing on criminals for reward. The most extraordinary was surely Jonathan Wild (1689–1725) who not only informed on criminals but actually organised robberies so that he could profit from the proceeds of the robberies as well as by 'grassing' on those who carried out the robberies and by charging victims for the return of stolen goods. He finally fell foul of the law and his execution at Tyburn in 1725 was a cause for rejoicing. His exploits formed the basis of John Gay's The Beggar's Opera *and Bertolt Brecht's* The Threepenny Opera.

Cops of brawn

Just as the City of London has guarded its independence from the wider Metropolitan authority, with its own Lord Mayor, so it has own police service, the City Police, which was formed in 1839. It has its own Commissioner entirely independent of the Metropolitan Police. Its headquarters is at Wood Street, on the former site of a Roman fort, and there are two other stations at Bishopsgate and Snow Hill. It has about 800 police officers (compared with 33,000 for the Met) and its own uniform with brass badges and buttons rather than the white of other police services; red and white chequered cap and sleeve bands (the colours of the City) are worn rather than the usual black and white. They are the reigning Olympic tug-of-war champions, having won the gold medal in 1920, the last time the event was included in the Olympics.

The White City
Once a temple of Olympic exertion – now shrine to consumerism

In 1908 a Hungarian impresario called Imre Kiralfy laid out 140 acres of ground in Wood Lane, London W12 to house a Franco-British Exhibition. The rather ugly concrete pavilions were whitewashed and soon given the name 'White City'. The Central London Railway (now the Central Line), recognising the opportunity to generate traffic from visitors to the exhibition, extended westwards the line which had opened in 1900 and opened White City Station. The exhibition was a modest success but Kiralfy and the Central received a bonus when the venue was used for the London Olympics. These should have been held in Rome but the untimely eruption of Vesuvius led the Italian government to announce that they could no longer accommodate the games.

The chairman of the British Olympic Association was the redoubtable Lord Desborough

Lottie Dod

(1855-1945) who had previously climbed the Matterhorn, rowed for Oxford in the Boat Race and swum across the base of Niagara falls – so re-scheduling the Olympics was for him a small matter. The 1908 London Olympics scored a number of 'firsts'. Thirty-seven women were allowed to compete, including the formidable British competitor Lottie Dod (1871-1960). Having won the Wimbledon ladies' singles title in 1887 at the age of fifteen (still a record) she won a silver medal for archery at the London Games while

her brother William won the gold medal in the men's event.

The Games left a permanent legacy in the Marathon. In the three previous Olympics the length of the race had varied slightly but King Edward VII requested that the race begin on the lawns of Windsor Castle so that his grandchildren, including the future Edward VIII and George VI, could watch. The route, via Stoke Poges and Wormwood Scrubs, finished in front of the royal box at White City, a distance of 26 miles 385 yards which became the standard for the event for future competitions. First to enter the stadium was an Italian confectioner called Dorando Pietri. Exhausted and disorientated he ran the wrong way round the track and collapsed. Faltering repeatedly, he was helped to the finishing line and, after protests from the perpetually chippy USA team, promptly disqualified. The following day Queen Alexandra presented Pietri with a silver cup as a consolation prize.

The end of culture
One legacy of the London games did not endure. During the games

the organisers agreed that in future medals would be awarded for architecture, sculpture and literature. At the 1912 Games, in Stockholm, the gold medal for literature was awarded, diplomatically, to the French aristocrat Pierre de Coubertin (1863–1937), who had been the moving spirit behind the revival of the Olympics (and strongly opposed the participation of women!). These awards were last made at the 1948 Games, also held in London. The White City Stadium was subsequently used as a venue for athletics and greyhound racing and was for a time the home of Queens Park Rangers football club. It is now the site of the Westfield Centre, Europe's largest shopping centre, selling everything from food and fashion to furniture and books.

COMETH THE HOUR COMETH THE MAN, RUNNING FAST

As the opening ceremony began for the 1948 London Olympics the British Team – which, as host nation, would enter the stadium last – discovered that its Union Flag had been left in an official's car. A young medical student who was assisting the official was despatched post-haste to retrieve it. His name was Roger Bannister. Needless to say, he made it in good time.

The manager of the British football team was Matt Busby, who handed out Craven A cigarettes at his team talk. Kenneth 'They think it's all over... it is now' Wolstenholme made one of his first match commentaries, during the England team's defeat by the flagrantly professional players of Yugoslavia.

HMS *Smallpox*
Some unusual London hospitals

B oats approaching the Port of London in 1881 were greeted by the sight (and smell) of three old ships moored in the Thames off Greenwich to accommodate the victims of smallpox, known to contemporaries as 'the loathsome disease'. The cries of sufferers as they scratched their pustules until they bled were accompanied by the smell they emitted. Eighty-five years earlier a Gloucestershire doctor, Edward Jenner, had demonstrated that smallpox could be prevented by vaccination with cowpox, a harmless condition, but such had been the opposition to the practice of being injected with an animal disease that many continued to succumb. An isolation hospital had been built in Hampstead in 1867 but when it began to fill with smallpox victims in an epidemic of 1870 the residents of the newly fashionable area were gripped by fear. They complained that ambulance crews bringing patients to the hospital stopped at the nearby pub, the Old Bull and Bush, thereby spreading the infection. The hospital survived and is now the famous Royal Free Hospital, but to avoid

The Old Bull and Bush

further controversy the authorities, in the form of the Metropolitan Asylums Board, transferred sufferers to the three converted ship hulks moored off Greenwich: the former battleship *Atlas*, the frigate *Endymion*, and the retired paddle-steamer *Castalia*. They remained there until 1902, performing very valuable service during which time more than 20,000 patients passed though them.

Edward Jenner

HOGARTH'S FAVOURITE BOOZER

The Old Bull and Bush is adjacent to Hampstead Heath close to the unused North End Station on the Northern Line. The building, which is Grade II listed, dates from the 17th century, one of its early patrons being the painter William

Hogarth (1697–1764) who was involved in creating its garden. It has traditionally attracted Cockneys visiting Hampstead Heath and it was this connection that led to its being celebrated in a song by music-hall star Florrie Forde called 'Down at the Old Bull and Bush'.

Ostensibly an even less likely contender for the role of hospital is St James's Palace, the fine Tudor building which was created by Henry VIII. For many years it was the principal residence of the sovereign and is still the official home of the Court of St James to which foreign ambassadors are accredited. Charles II and Queen Anne were both born there and it is the home of Princess Anne, the Princess Royal. However, it was a hospital long before it became a palace. It may date from before the Norman Conquest and was certainly in use in the reign of Henry II (1154–89). By the 15th century it had become a leper hospital for young women run by nuns of the Augustinian order and was given by Henry VI to his new foundation, Eton College. The dissolution of the religious houses led to its acquisition by Henry VIII for his new palace.

Jest a hospital

London's oldest hospital is St Bartholomew's (Barts as it is better known), situated close to the meat market at Smithfield. It was founded by Rahere, a court jester to Henry I, who had suffered an attack of malaria on a pilgrimage to Rome and as a result saw a vision of St Bartholomew telling him to found a hospital at the Smooth Field (Smithfield). The only surviving part of Rahere's

Rahere's tomb

original foundation is the fine little church of St Bartholomew-the-Great which contains Rahere's tomb and once accommodated a print works where future great American polymath Benjamin Franklin worked as a typesetter. Nearby is the equally interesting St Bartholomew-the-Less, founded in 1184 as a chapel to the hospital.

Barts is part of the Barts and The London NHS Trust, its partner in the trust being the Royal London Hospital in Whitechapel. The Royal London was founded in 1740 as the London Infirmary and its medical school was the first in England, founded in 1785. Perhaps the hospital's most famous resident was Joseph Merrick (1862-90), the so-called 'Elephant Man', whose deformities attracted the sympathy of Sir Frederick Treves (1853-1923) who rescued Merrick from a freak show in Belgium and found him a home at the hospital. Merrick was the subject of the film *The Elephant Man* (1980), with John Hurt in the title role.

The Maiden Tribute of Modern Babylon
The Pall Mall Gazette

The *Pall Mall Gazette* was founded in 1865, taking its name from a fictional newspaper featured in the work of the writer William Makepeace Thackeray. It never had any connection with the street from which it took its name and was initially conservative in tone. This changed when WT

WT Stead

Stead joined the magazine in 1880, becoming editor in 1883. Under Stead it became a campaigning journal, arousing the criticism of one of its contributors, Matthew Arnold, at the 'Americanisation' of British journalism. Other writers included Oscar Wilde, George Bernard Shaw, HG Wells, Rudyard Kipling and Robert Louis Stevenson. Stead became associated with a group known as the Social Purity Movement, amongst whom was Josephine Butler, who sought to improve the treatment of women and children in Victorian Britain. Bramwell Booth of the Salvation Army and Rebecca Jarrett, a reformed prostitute, were also members. Stead decided to demonstrate that, in Victorian London, it was possible to purchase a child for immoral purposes. Through Rebecca Jarrett, Stead made contact with the alcoholic mother of 13-year-old Eliza Armstrong who lived in Lisson Grove. On 3rd June 1885, Stead purchased the child for £5 and handed her over to Bramwell Booth who took the child to France where she was cared for by members of the Salvation Army.

LONDON'S OLDEST MULTI-STOREY CAR PARK

The child–buying bargain was sealed in Poland Street, a harmless looking thoroughfare in Soho now inhabited by garment trades and media organisations. Thrillingly, it also includes Britain's oldest multi-storey car park, opened in 1934 and still thriving today.

On Monday, 6th July, under the heading 'The Maiden Tribute of Modern Babylon', Stead published the first instalment of the story which, with salacious sub-headings like 'The Violation of Virgins', drew attention to the ease with which it was possible to abuse young children. WH Smith and sons refused to handle the magazine because of its sensational and pornographic character but volunteers, including the Salvation Army and George Bernard Shaw, distributed and sold the issue. The Home Secretary pleaded with Stead to cease publication of further details of the affair. Stead replied that the government would first have to pass a Bill, which had stalled in the House of Commons, raising the age of sexual consent from 13 to 16. The Bill was duly passed but in the meantime Stead's enemies, including other newspapers who were jealous of his success, were gathering their forces.

Titanic loss

Stead, Jarrett and Bramwell Booth were prosecuted for abducting Eliza, the case turning on the legal technicality that Eliza had been acquired with the permission of the mother but not her father. Booth was acquitted, Jarrett sentenced to six months and Stead to three months. He continued to edit the *Gazette* from his cell in Holloway of which he said, 'Never had I a pleasanter holiday, a more charming season of repose.' He was allowed to keep his prison uniform and on 10th November each year, the anniversary of his conviction, he wore it to remind readers of his 'triumph'. Stead died in April 1912 in the *Titanic* disaster, last seen helping others into the lifeboats and making no attempt to save himself. In 1923 the *Pall Mall Gazette* was absorbed by the *Evening Standard* which continues to flourish.

THE *STRAND MAGAZINE* – STRANDED BUT REFLOATED

An equally famous London publication was the **Strand Magazine** *which was first published in 1891 from Burleigh Street, off the Strand, carrying illustrated pieces from some of the leading writers of the day, including Kipling, Tolstoy, Churchill and Chesterton. It became famous for its publication in serial form of Arthur Conan Doyle's Sherlock Holmes stories, crowds gathering outside the magazine's offices for the latest instalment. It closed in 1950 but was revived in 1998 with stories by John Mortimer and Ruth Rendell among others.*

Lifeblood of London
The capital's power stations

Many of London's most glorious examples of industrial architecture have been its power stations, some of which have since found other uses. They were built on the banks of the Thames to facilitate delivery by river of the large quantities of coal that they required. The most famous is Bankside Power Station designed by Sir Giles Gilbert Scott who also designed the famous British red telephone box. It was specified that the central chimney, 99 metres high, should be lower than the spire of St Paul's Cathedral directly across the Thames. It is close to the site of 'Shakespeare's Globe' theatre which opened in 1997. Power generation began there in 1952 though the complex was not completed until 1963. In 1981 generation ceased and in 1993 it narrowly escaped demolition by developers when a BBC programme, *One Foot in the Past*, inspired a campaign to preserve it. In 1994 it was acquired by the trustees of the Tate Gallery and in 2000, after substantial construction works, it opened as Tate Modern. The original Tate Gallery (financed by the Tate & Lyle sugar family) became known as Tate Britain.

Giles Gilbert Scott designed an older and larger power station at Battersea in the 1930s, the first large power station designed to provide

The Tate Modern

electricity over a wide area. It began to generate electricity in 1933 and was enlarged in the 1950s. In 1983 power generation ceased and since that time a number of plans to redevelop the site (shopping malls, apartments, theme parks, etc) have come and gone without success. Its imposing structure has featured in iconic artwork for the successful British band Pink Floyd, as well as a number of episodes of *Doctor Who* and similar entertainments. It is now in the process of being converted into a shopping and entertainment centre with one-bedroomed apartments costing from £600,000.

Power to the People!

In the 1880s Sebastian di Ferranti, who was descended from the Doges

Lots Road Power Station

Lots Road Power Station, on Chelsea Creek, was opened on the banks of the Thames in 1905 to provide power to the newly electrified London Underground railway lines. It was built by the flamboyant American entrepreneur Charles Tyson Yerkes and remained in use until 2002 when the Underground started to take its power from the National Grid. It was featured in a famous World War II poster titled 'The Proud City' as a symbol of London's defiance during the Blitz, accompanied by a quotation from the American painter James McNeill Whistler: 'the poor buildings lose themselves in the dim sky and the tall chimneys become campanili...' Ironically, Whistler had died in 1903 protesting against the construction of the station.

of Venice through his father and a Liverpudlian photographer on his mother's side, supplied power to premises in and around Bond Street from a small generator in the Grosvenor Gallery, Bond Street, the electricity being distributed through cables trailing across rooftops. In 1890 he opened what was then the world's largest power station in Deptford. A fortnight later the transformer room burst into flames; nonetheless the station remained in use until 1953. The site has since been redeveloped as housing, the nearby Ferranti Park reminding residents of its origins.

At about the same time Greenwich Power Station was commissioned by the London County Council to provide electricity for London's trams. After these ceased to run it was used to supply standby power for Lots Road and it remains in use as a back-up station, near the site of the Millennium Dome.

AC/DC IN SUBURBAN RAILWAY SHOCK

The construction of Lots Road was accompanied by an argument between Yerkes and the irascible chairman of the Metropolitan Railway, Sir Edward Watkin, about the relative merits of direct and alternating current. Watkin built his own station, assuring his shareholders that with direct current no motor was necessary, the current passing straight to the wheels! At one point the government,

Sir Edward William Watkin

faced with the claims of rival schemes to supply electricity to London, called in as arbitrator an Old Etonian who was an authority on the rules of Association Football.

Gone but not forgotten
The Festival Hall's lost companions

In 1951 a previously derelict site on the South Bank of the Thames on either side of Hungerford Bridge was transformed into a site for the Festival of Britain, an enterprise masterminded by Herbert Morrison, a prominent member of the Labour government, to commemorate the centenary of the Great Exhibition. It was also intended to cheer people up at a time of post-war austerity and to attract tourists, especially Americans with their much-needed dollars. Its most prominent buildings

The Skylon

were the Royal Festival Hall, to the east of Hungerford Bridge, which survives; and the Dome of Discovery and the Skylon to the west of the bridge, which do not. The latter was a cigar-shaped tubular tower, 250 feet high, coming to a point at each end. Its steel frame was covered in aluminium panels. Designed by the young architects Philip Powell and Hidalgo Moya it appeared to defy the laws of gravity since it rested on a platform of barely visible wires 40 feet above the ground. A few days before the Festival was officially opened by King George VI a student scaled the Skylon and attached a

Sherlock Holmes and Dr Watson

University of London scarf to the top. It was removed before the royal party arrived. When the exhibition ended it was dismantled in 1952 (the new Prime Minister, Winston Churchill, thought it was 'three-dimensional socialist propaganda') and some of it was turned into paper knives by the 600 Group scrap merchants of 600, Commercial Road, London who gave them to customers as souvenirs. A portion of it came to rest in the garden of Hidalgo Moya's home in Rye, Sussex while a further small section was traced as recently as January 2011 in the possession of Nick Baughan, a descendant of a director of the 600 Group. The Skylon has given its name to a number of ambitious structures, notably to a restaurant near Niagara Falls. The origin of the name is the subject of many legends but it was probably cooked up in the architects' office. At the time names ending in 'on' were regarded as futuristic, like the new textiles nylon and rayon.

Nearby, the Dome of Discovery was a circular building, 365 feet in diameter, topped by a dome-shaped aluminium roof. At the time of its

The Sherlock Holmes Museum

construction it was the largest dome in the world and, like its Victorian predecessor the Crystal Palace, it was designed as a temporary structure. It contained galleries featuring new discoveries and inventions ranging from the exploration of outer space to new techniques for making sheet glass, together with a reconstruction of Sherlock Holmes's fictional flat at 221B Baker Street. Though derided at the time as a waste of precious building materials, ten million visitors paid to attend the festival (far more than visited the Millennium Dome in 2000) and the London County Council pocketed a handsome profit. The Dome followed the Skylon into demolition to make way for the Shell Centre, Jubilee Gardens and, in 2000, the London Eye ferris

wheel. Only Sherlock Holmes's flat survived, transported to a pub in Northumberland Street, just across the river near Charing Cross.

The London Eye, opened on 31st December 1999 to celebrate the turn of the millennium, was originally intended to close after five years. The largest ferris wheel in Europe at 135 metres in height, it is Britain's most popular tourist attraction and is used by over 3.8 million people each year. It has probably become a permanent feature of London's skyline.

'IS SHERLOCK HOLMES AT HOME?'

221B Baker Street has never existed as an address but since its first appearance in 1887 in A Study in Scarlet *people have been addressing letters to it. Much scholarly effort has been devoted to identifying its whereabouts even though, when Conan Doyle wrote the Sherlock Holmes stories, the numbers along the street ran only to 100. The Abbey National Building Society long occupied the site where 221B would have been and is said to have employed someone whose sole task was to answer letters addressed to the famous detective. In 1990 the Sherlock Homes Museum, at 239 Baker Street, unveiled a plaque declaring that it was 'officially' number 221B.*

Meat, veg, coarse language and fences
The offerings of London's lively markets

London has an unrivalled selection of markets, some of them dating from Roman times. Leadenhall Market in the City dates from that period though it takes its name from a house with a lead roof which was situated in the vicinity in the 14th century. Both were burned down in the Great Fire of 1666 and the market was most recently developed in 1881 when the present structures were constructed by the City architect, Sir Horace Jones, to sell meat, poultry, vegetables, plants and fish, recently joined by a selection of cafes, restaurants, bookshops and the ubiquitous wine bars. In 1851-66 Jones had built the meat market at

Smithfield Market

Smithfield to replace the live cattle market which had flourished in the area since the 12th century but was, by the 19th century, a scene of mayhem with live cattle, goaded by crowds, running wild in shops and giving us the phrase 'bull in a china shop'. Billingsgate, originally sited close to the Monument in the heart of the City, is recorded as trading in 1016, selling corn, malt and salt as well as fish. It quickly acquired a reputation for foul language which it retained after its move to the vicinity of Canary Wharf on the Isle of Dogs in 1982. Its former building – designed, like Smithfield, by Sir Horace Jones – is now the trading floor of an international bank, where no doubt the language employed is of a more salubrious nature.

London is also well supplied with street markets, one of the most famous being the Sunday market in Middlesex Street, Whitechapel, which was first referred to as Peticote Lane on a map of 1608. In the late 17th century it was settled by Jewish traders, who had been welcomed back to England in the 1650s by Oliver Cromwell after being expelled by Edward I in 1290, and by Huguenot silk weavers fleeing the persecutions of Louis XIV in France. It was at this time that it became strongly associated with the sale of textiles and clothing. In the early 20th century the authorities tried to stop Sunday trading by driving fire engines through the crowd but the market prospered and spread to nearby streets like Brick Lane, with almost

Billingsgate Fish Market

1,000 separate stalls. Portobello Road Market in Notting Hill also trades on Sunday mornings, beginning in the 1870s amongst gypsies who came to buy and sell horses and herbs. To these were later added costermongers but after World War II the character of the market changed and it began an antiques market, which it remains.

DEALER IN DEATH

Near to Portobello Road Market was 10, Rillington Place where John Christie murdered as many as eight women over a ten-year period before being hanged at Pentonville in 1954. In the meantime Timothy Evans had been hanged for one of the murders. The notorious street was renamed Ruston Close. It was demolished in the 1970s and made way for Bartle Road.

Del Boy paradise

Perhaps the most intriguing of London's markets is Bermondsey Market, officially called New Caledonian Market just off Tower Bridge Road in Southwark. Normally a person buying goods that were later shown to be stolen would forfeit them if the owner claimed them but Bermondsey was the last of London's Marchés Ouverts where stolen goods could be sold between sunrise and sunset with good title passing from buyer to seller. The market became a very popular outlet for antiques. In 1995 the ancient law of Marché Ouvert was abolished and this outlet for 'fenced' goods was lost.

Usurers by any other name
The pawnbrokers of Lombard Street

In the Middle Ages 'usury', or lending money for interest, was forbidden by the Christian church. Consequently banking, an essential function in the promotion of trade, was dominated by Jews who were not

Lombard Street

subject to the laws of the church. This was used as an explanation for their unpopularity and also accounted for their expulsion from England in 1290 by Edward I, who owed them money. Into the breach stepped a group of merchants from Lombardy, the region around Milan in northern Italy. They managed to circumvent the laws of the church by becoming, in effect, pawnbrokers. They would advance money against the security of objects of value (jewellery, gold or fine cloth) and would return the items for rather more than they had loaned – interest by another name. They settled in a street in London which still bears the name Lombard Street and came to contain the headquarters of many major banks.

Nearby, in Threadneedle Street, is the Bank of England which was set up in 1694 by two City merchants, William Paterson and Michael Godfrey, to finance William III's wars against Louis XIV. Instead of debasing the currency as other monarchs had done when they were short of money, William III guaranteed an interest payment of 8 per cent to those who loaned money to the government via the bank, the loans being underwritten by a 'Tunnage' tax levied on alcohol and shipping. Over £1.2 million was raised in 11 days. The bank was known for many years as the 'Tunnage Bank' and William further emphasised his commitment to sound money by having new coinage issued by the Royal Mint under the wardenship of Sir Isaac Newton who ruthlessly pursued any forgers. The Bank of England quickly gained a reputation as a sound investment. It was originally based at Mercers' Hall off Cheapside and moved to its present site in 1734. The government's (no doubt dwindling) reserves of gold bullion and foreign currency are kept in its vaults.

EXPENSIVE CHICKENFEED

Poultry Street, at the east end of Cheapside near the Bank of England, reminds us of the market that traded there in the Middle Ages. In 1939 it became the headquarters of the Midland Bank, then the largest in the world. On the ground floor was the world's most magnificent bank branch, designed by Sir Edwin Lutyens, giving new meaning to the expression marble halls. In 2015, after standing idle for 7 years, builders moved in to convert the building into a luxury hotel.

Hammerbeams and Hoovers
Art Deco in London

London has many Art Deco buildings but two of them have extraordinary origins. The movement originated in France and reached a climax in 1925 with the Exposition Internationale des Arts Décoratifs et Industriels Modernes in Paris. The movement emphasised bold colours and geometric shapes in contrast to the earlier Art Nouveau with pastel shades and sweeping curves. Eltham Palace, a few miles from Greenwich in southeast London, is the unlikely site of one of Britain's

Eltham Palace

most striking Art Deco designs. The Palace is recorded in the *Domesday Book* of 1086 as belonging to the brother of William the Conqueror and during the following centuries it was turned into a magnificent royal palace with an outstanding hammerbeam roof dating from 1479. Henry VIII added a chapel and both he and his daughter, the future Elizabeth I, spent many years here during childhood. The construction of Greenwich Palace nearby led to its abandonment by the royal family and by the 20th century much of it was in ruins, the great hall being used as a barn.

In 1931 Eltham Palace was purchased by Stephen and Virginia Courtauld, textile millionaires, who restored the hall, laid out the gardens and constructed a magnificent Art Deco mansion adjacent to the hall. Some of its features have been compared to those of an ocean liner of the period together with such characteristic Art Deco features as maple veneered walls, a shining aluminium leaf ceiling and an onyx bath. In 1995 the estate was acquired by English Heritage who restored the interiors and introduced additional furniture of the period.

New broom at Tesco

An even more astonishing site for an Art Deco building is to be found at Perivale, on Western Avenue, in the form of the Hoover Building. Built in 1932 as a factory with offices, the façade has white columns which frame long green-painted windows with bands of dark blue and red. The interior is also in the Art Deco style and, as demand for vacuum cleaners grew, the building gradually expanded up to the eve of World War II by which time it employed 600 people. During the war the factory manufactured components for aircraft and tanks. In 1986 it was closed and there were fears that it would suffer the fate of the nearby Firestone factory, also Art Deco, which had been demolished by developers a day before campaigners obtained a listed building order. In 1989 Tesco came to the rescue when they bought the Hoover site, built a supermarket at the rear in a style sympathetic to the Hoover building and restored the original building as offices.

'A roost for every bird'
Philanthropy and London's poor

London's government struggled to provide decent housing for the sevenfold increase in its population which occurred in the 19th century but a significant contribution was made by individual philanthropists. The first of these was George Peabody (1795-1869) who was born in Massachusetts but moved to London in the 1830s where he founded a bank which was the ancestor of the JP Morgan bank. In 1862 he founded the Peabody Trust to provide improved housing for working-class people. The Trust insisted that all its residents be vaccinated, thus giving impetus to the controversial campaign to eradicate smallpox. The Fabian writer Beatrice Potter (later Beatrice Webb, 1858-1943), when writing in 1887 about the poor living conditions endured by casual workers in the London docks, commented that dockers chose to live at a distance in places like Hackney and Forest Gate unless they could find a 'Peabody' whose dwellings offered a refuge from the surrounding squalor. In the 21st century the Peabody Trust owns or manages nearly 20 thousand properties across 30 London boroughs, housing about 50 thousand people, including the new residences in Boxley Street, Canning Town. Upon his death in 1869 Peabody, with the consent of Queen Victoria, was temporarily interred in Westminster Abbey before his remains were taken to America by the Royal Navy where he was buried in the town of his birth, Danvers, Massachusetts, which changed its name to Peabody in his honour.

The ornate drinking fountain

The Victoria Park fountain

Angela Georgina Burdett-Coutts

in Victoria Park, Hackney, is one reminder of the work of Angela Burdett-Coutts (1814-1906). She was the daughter of the radical politician Sir Frances Burdett (1770-1844) who had married Sophia Coutts of the wealthy banking family. In 1837, aged 23, Angela became the wealthiest woman in England when she inherited her grandfather's fortune. The word 'eccentric' does little justice to one who, as a young woman, proposed (unsuccessfully) to the aged Duke of Wellington and who at the age of 66 married her 29-year-old secretary William Bartlett – a union described by Queen Victoria as 'positively distressing and ridiculous'.

Angela used her St James's Square home to entertain such figures as William Gladstone, Michael Faraday, Charles Babbage and Charles Dickens who dedicated his novel *Martin Chuzzlewit* to her memory and encouraged her to found many 'ragged' schools for poor children. Her main contributions to the welfare of the poor comprised the establishment of a hostel for homeless women, Urania Cottage in Shepherd's Bush (which she planned with Charles Dickens); and the construction of model dwellings at Nova Scotia Gardens, Bethnal Green, in place of the foul tenements that had existed before in this most notorious corner of London, a haunt of body-snatchers known as The Jago. She also paid for the creation of drinking fountains providing clean water, an important benefit for those who could not afford a piped supply. Of these the most prominent and spectacular is the one in Victoria Park, Hackney.

Out-of-step Jack

Montagu William Lowry-Corry (1838-1903) was a grandson of the Earl of Shaftesbury from whom he inherited his philanthropic genes. In 1880, after serving as private secretary to Benjamin Disraeli, Corry was created Baron Rowton and in 1890 he set up a trust to build and run decent common lodging houses for working men. The first Rowton House opened in Vauxhall in 1892 and in its first year over 140,000 beds were let at sixpence a night, offering such facilities as clean sheets, washrooms and hot water, the last a rare luxury. Five other Rowton houses followed, of which the best known was Tower House in Fieldgate Street, Whitechapel which housed some notable residents. Jack London (1876-1916) described Tower house as 'the Monster Doss House' in *The People of the Abyss* (1903) and recorded that it was 'full of life that was degrading and unwholesome' but other commentators were kinder. Thirty years later, in *Down and Out in Paris and London* George Orwell (1903-50) wrote of Tower House that: 'The best lodging houses are the Rowton houses where the charge is a shilling, for which you get a cubicle to yourself and the use of excellent bathrooms. You can also pay half a crown for a special, which is practically hotel accommodation. The Rowton houses are splendid buildings and the only objection to them is the strict discipline with rules against cooking, card playing etc.'

STALIN'S YOUTH HOSTELLING DAYS

Tower House's most notorious resident left no record of his impressions though the fact that he spent a fortnight there in 1907 suggests that he appreciated the standard of accommodation it offered. He registered as Iosif Dzhugashvili but is better known as Joseph Stalin. He rented a sixpence-a-night cubicle while attending the fifth congress of the Russian Social Democratic and Labour Party in Whitechapel. That building has since been converted into luxury flats and the only Rowton House still used for its original purpose is 220, Arlington Road, Camden – opened in 1905 and known as 'Dracula's Castle' or, for its largely Irish patrons, as 'The Mickey'.

City of God?
London's places of worship

The churches of Sir Christopher Wren – those that survived the Blitz – are familiar to most Londoners but those places of worship of other denominations and faiths are perhaps not as well known as they deserve. One of the most controversial in its day was the Roman Catholic Westminster Cathedral. The restoration of the Catholic

Westminster Cathedral

The Church of St Sophia

hierarchy by the appointment of Cardinal Wiseman as Archbishop of Westminster in 1850 (the first since the Reformation) was itself seen as a threat to the supremacy of the Church of England and it was not until 1884 that Cardinal Manning, Wiseman's successor, bought the site for a new cathedral in Francis Street near Victoria Station. The building is striking, with contrasting bands of brick and Portland stone while the interior is ablaze with mosaics in the Byzantine style using 100 different kinds of marble. The eight dark green columns which form the widest nave in England were taken from the same quarry as provided the marble for the Hagia Sophia in Istanbul 1,300 years earlier. Less controversial was St Peter's Italian church in Clerkenwell, built in 1863 at the request of the Italian statesman Mazzini to accommodate the growing Italian community in London. Its narrow but striking façade on the Clerkenwell Road arguably does less than justice to its beautiful interior decoration.

Another St Sophia, less grand than that of Istanbul, is to be found in Moscow Road, Bayswater. It was completed in 1882 by John Scott, the son of Sir George Gilbert Scott (architect of St Pancras Station and the Albert Memorial) to serve the Greek Orthodox community which

The Italian church of St Peter

grew in London after Greece gained its independence from Ottoman Turkey in 1832. Its richly furnished interior and icon paintings are striking.

The Russian Orthodox presence is much older, dating from the visit to London of Peter the Great in 1698 when a church was attached to the Russian Embassy. After many moves (and schisms within the Russian Orthodox community) a permanent home for the congregation was found in Harvard Road, Chiswick. In 2005 the new Russian Cathedral was consecrated, its prominent blue 'onion dome' surmounted by a golden cross bringing a little piece of Russia to this quiet corner of London. The cathedral is dedicated to 'The Holy Royal Martyrs of Russia'.

Other faiths are also represented in London, often by spectacular buildings. One of the most striking is the Shri Swaminarayan Mandir, better known as the Neasden Temple. The site was acquired in 1990 and consignments of Bulgarian limestone and Italian Carrara marble began to be shipped to India where they were carved into over 26,000 components

The Neasden Temple

for the temple. It was opened in 1995, covering 1.5 acres with space for 5,000 Hindu worshippers, its shining white domes and pinnacles visible for miles.

London's best-known mosque is the London Central Mosque (often referred to as the Regent's Park Mosque) which was completed in 1978 adjacent to the Islamic cultural centre which was opened by King George VI in 1944 as a gift from the people of Britain to its Muslim community. Its gold dome is a prominent feature of the building which has a capacity of 5,000 worshippers. The East London Mosque in Whitechapel, less often frequented by visitors to London, is

equally large and has a longer history. Its construction was first mooted at a meeting at the Ritz Hotel in 1910 by prominent Muslims who wanted a suitable building in which to practise their religion. The Aga Khan was an early patron. Whitechapel was an obvious site because land was relatively inexpensive and the area had a large, albeit transient, Muslim population of seamen coming into the London docks. A striking feature of Whitechapel Road, the mosque opened in 1985 and lies adjacent to the Jewish Great Synagogue in Fieldgate Street which opened in 1899.

The London Central Mosque

THE OUT-OF-POCKET QUAKER

In the 19th century there were many Jews living in Whitechapel, refugees from persecution in Russia. There were also many synagogues but the oldest in Britain is a short distance from Whitechapel at Bevis Marks in the City. The synagogue was built in 1699 for the Iberian Jewish community by Joseph Avis, a Quaker, who agreed to build it for £2,750 but later declined the fee on the grounds that it was immoral to profit from the building of a house of God.

Empire of the bun
Lyons Teashops and Corner Houses

From 1894 to 1981 no day out in London was complete unless it included a cup of tea (or occasionally coffee) and a piece of cake at a Lyons teashop with its distinctive gold lettering on a white background. The company was founded in 1887 as a spin-off from the Salmon and Gluckstein tobacco business. Nigella Lawson, the food writer and TV chef, is descended from the Salmon family. The tearooms offered cheap, standardised menus which were served by waitresses known as 'Nippies', the business taking its name from Joseph Nathaniel Lyons who ran the business from its earliest days. Most of the food was produced at the firm's headquarters at Cadby Hall in Hammersmith. The company made its own cakes and also ice cream under the name Lyons Maid. In addition to the teashops Lyons opened Lyons Corner Houses in the Strand, Coventry Street and Oxford Street and two Maisons Lyons at Marble Arch and Shaftesbury Avenue. They were noted for their attractive Art Deco interiors on four or five storeys with bright lighting. They had a well-stocked food hall on the ground floor and restaurants of different character on the upper storeys: a brasserie, a grill room, the first Wimpy bars, an egg and bacon room (popular with students because of its swift service and wide variety of good food) and similar facilities to suit all tastes. As early as 1895 Lyons acquired a lease on the Trocadero music hall at the bottom of Shaftesbury Avenue and built an elaborately decorated restaurant notable for its famous Long Bar in multi-coloured marble. The company also ran some large hotels including the Cumberland at Marble Arch and the Tower Hotel near the Tower of London.

A PC OF CAKE?

J Lyons and Company was the first British firm to use programmable computers in its businesses, in processing orders from its shops and payroll for its staff and from 1947-63 manufactured and sold LEO (Lyons Electronic Office) computers.

In the 1960s the restaurants began to lose money in the face of mounting competition from other chains and the company's fortunes were further damaged by some unwise speculation in foreign currencies. The last Corner House closed in 1977 and the last tearoom in 1981 while its own branded products were sold off to other manufacturers. The Trocadero became a complex of shops, restaurants and entertainments including The Guinness World of Records but this, and subsequent

ventures, were not financially successful and the building is being converted into a budget hotel, possibly accompanied by a TK Maxx outlet. In 1978 Lyons was acquired by Allied Breweries and became part of Allied Lyons, a drinks company. Its demise coincided with the rise of companies like McDonald's and Starbucks who filled the gap left by Lyons, though at much higher prices.

Wren, Rutherford – and Ribbentrop
Patrons of London's learned establishments

London is well furnished with organisations dedicated to the advancement of learning and the arts and many of them enjoy royal patronage. The most eminent is surely the Royal Society for the promotion of science and mathematics. It was formally constituted in 1660 at a meeting at Gresham College which was attended by, amongst others, the physicist Robert Boyle and the astronomer, later architect, Christopher Wren. In 1662 it received a charter from Charles

II and from its earliest days it was active in promoting scientific research including, for example, the exploratory voyages of Captain Cook. A Fellowship of the Royal Society is the most coveted honour that a scientist can achieve short of a Nobel Prize and to list its presidents is to compile a roll of honour of the most eminent scientists who have ever lived. They include Christopher Wren, Isaac Newton and Ernest Rutherford. In 1967 the Royal Society moved to its present home at 8-9, Carlton House Terrace, built by John Nash after the demolition of Carlton House. From 1849 until World War II the building was the home of the German Embassy, its last ambassador being the despised Joachim von Ribbentrop, a former champagne salesman who was hanged as a war criminal. The building, which has retained much of its 1930s décor, is sometimes opened to the public, notably during the Summer Science Exhibitions which are held in July. In 1902 the British Academy was founded to do for the humanities what the Royal Society does for science. It founders included Leslie Stephen, father of Virginia Woolf , and the then Prime Minister AJ Balfour. It is to be found at 10, Carlton House Terrace, next door to the Royal Society.

The Royal Society is sometimes confused with the Royal Society of Arts whose full title is the Royal Society for the Encouragement of Arts, Manufactures and Commerce, based at John Adam Street near Charing Cross. Its was founded in 1754 by a drawing master from Northampton, William Shipley, and received great impetus when it received its royal charter in 1847 while Prince Albert was President. It was very active in organising the Great Exhibition of 1851 and instituted the process by which blue plaques are placed on buildings

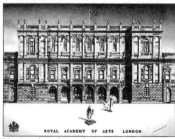

The Royal Academy of Arts in London

associated with famous people; the first, in 1867, was affixed on the house in Holles Street, Mayfair, where the poet George Byron (1788-1824) was born. The house was later demolished. The blue plaque scheme is now administered by English Heritage.

THE ADELPHI ADAMS

Almost opposite the Royal Society of Arts in John Adam Street is Adelphi Terrace. In the 1770s the brothers John, Robert, James and William Adam built an imposing row of terraced houses overlooking the Thames called The Adelphi, the Greek word for brothers. It was surrounded by four streets named after the brothers. The narrowing of the Thames to form Victoria Embankment Gardens deprived the terrace of its riverside site and in the 1930s the terrace was demolished, a new building erected (still called Adelphi) and the streets renamed. John Adam Street survives together with Robert Street and Lower Robert Street – London's only street which is entirely underground, leading from Robert Street to Savoy Place.

Lollipops and candles

The Royal Academy of Arts was founded in 1768 during the reign of George III who declared that he would be its 'patron, protector and supporter'. In 1769 the Academy moved into the new Somerset House though many of its early exhibitions were held at the Foundling Hospital which enjoyed the patronage of early members like Sir Joshua Reynolds and William Hogarth. After a brief stay in Trafalgar Square the Academy moved in 1868 to Burlington House in Piccadilly where it remains. There it holds its Summer Exhibitions when about 1,200 works are exhibited from entries submitted by about 10,000 hopeful artists whose ambition is to feature in this famous event. Winston Churchill had paintings selected for the exhibition on several occasions.

The Royal Academy of Music was first proposed in 1774 by the musician Charles Burney who wanted to convert the Foundling Hospital into a musical academy. This was defeated but in 1822 the proposal was revived at a meeting at the Thatched House Tavern in St James's Street and in 1823 it opened in premises near Hanover Square with 21 pupils, one of them being the 12-year-old Fanny Dickens, sister of Charles. The Academy received its royal charter in 1830 but struggled financially until Gladstone's government gave it an annual grant of £500 in 1864. In 1912 it moved into its present premises in Marylebone Road where it continues to flourish. It is Britain's oldest degree-giving music school and is now a college of the University of London, giving regular concerts to which the public are admitted. Its former pupils include Sir John Barbirolli, Sir Simon Rattle, Dame Evelyn Glennie and Sir Elton John.

Acting up in Theatreland
Life beyond the fringe

In Shakespeare's time, and for long after, actors and theatres were as welcome as neighbours as were prostitutes and bawdy houses. For this reason London's entertainment district was centred on Bankside, across London Bridge and safely distant from the respectable areas north of the river that were more concerned with commerce. There the theatres could keep company with bordellos and bear baiting. North of the Thames the Curtain Theatre, opened in 1577, lay in Shoreditch just outside the City boundary and was used by Shakespeare's company, the Lord Chamberlain's Men, to produce *Henry V* and *Romeo and Juliet*, the latter received with 'Curtain plaudits' (great enthusiasm). It was destroyed in the Great Fire and a plaque marks its site at Hewett Street, off Curtain Road. The Blackfriars Theatre also opened in 1577 within the City, its status protected by the fact that its proprietor, Richard Farrant, was also Master of the Music at Windsor and claimed that its primary use was to train boys for the king's choir. It was closed by the Puritans in 1642 and demolished in 1665 but its memory lives on in its site, now named Playhouse Yard. The only theatre now within the City is The Mermaid at Puddle Dock, Upper Thames Street. It was the brainchild of (later Sir) Bernard Miles, opening as a temporary theatre at the Royal Exchange to mark the coronation of Queen Elizabeth

II in 1953 and was so successful that the City Corporation granted 'Bernard Miles and other Poor Players of London' a lease on a derelict Victorian warehouse which became a permanent structure in 1959.

FOR FOLIO'S SAKE

Just off Aldermanbury, in front of the City's Guildhall Library, is a quiet little garden dedicated to the memory of John Heming and Henry Condell, friends and colleagues of Shakespeare who, in 1623, compiled an edition of 36 of Shakespeare's plays in the famous **First Folio.** *It also contained a likeness of the poet. Without their work many of the plays would surely have been lost for ever.*

The first theatre on Bankside was The Rose which was built by an impresario and property developer called Philip Henslowe in 1587 and was the location of the first productions of Marlowe's *Tamburlaine* and Shakespeare's *Henry VI, Part I.* Its success was such that it was soon followed, and eclipsed, by The Swan and The Globe, also on Bankside. It was forgotten until construction

Shakespeare's Globe Theatre

work revealed its foundations and ground plan close to Southwark Bridge where there is now an exhibition. Philip Henslowe features as a prominent character, played by Geoffrey Rush, in the 1998 film *Shakespeare in Love.* The Globe in fact began life in 1576 close to the later site of The Curtain in what is now Curtain Road. It was built by the actor James Burbage and prospered but after a dispute with the owner of the land on which it stood Burbage and his company dismantled it one night, moved it across the river and re-erected it as The Globe in 1599, one of the shareholders being William Shakespeare who was presumably also one of the removal men. Like many theatres of the time it had a relatively short life and was destroyed by fire in 1613 during a performance of *Henry VIII* when an enterprising special effects man fired two cannon to welcome the arrival of the actor playing the king. These set fire to the thatch and the theatre was destroyed. The only casualty was a man whose breeches caught fire and who 'put it out with bottled ale'.

The construction of a replica of Shakespeare's Globe was due to the enterprise of the American actor Sam Wanamaker who died in 1993 before the project was completed. Having seen a replica of the original theatre at a fair in Chicago as a young man he came to London to see the original and was shocked to find that it no longer existed. The actual site of the original Globe is nearby and its foundations may be seen in the courtyard of some flats on Park Street.

A special, if bizarre, place in the history of theatre is reserved for a much later structure, the Theatre Royal, Haymarket, built in 1720. Henry Fielding became its manager in 1735 and proceeded to produce a series of plays which satirised the Prime Minister Sir Robert Walpole as a cynical swindler. The government attempted to prosecute the proprietor of the theatre under the 1714 Vagrancy Act, taking advantage of the fact that the Act enabled actors to be classed as vagrants. The defence argued that, as the freeholder of a substantial property – the theatre – the proprietor, whose name was John Harper, was clearly not a vagrant. They further argued that he was unsuitable for the normal penalty for vagrancy, hard labour, because 'he being so corpulent, it is not possible for him either to labour, or to wander a great deal'. Enraged, in 1737 Walpole passed the Theatrical Licensing Act which made the Lord Chamberlain responsible for issuing licences to theatres and for licensing plays before they could be staged. The office survived until 1968.

He was in charge

Other theatres have less controversial histories. One of the most famous throughout the world is the London Palladium in Argyll Street near Oxford Circus. It opened as a music hall in 1910 with over 2,000 seats and made the careers of a number of entertainers as well as featuring many established stars like Judy Garland, The Beatles and Danny

The London Palladium

Kaye whose show in 1948 was so popular that special arrangements had to be made to obtain tickets for King George VI, Queen Elizabeth and the two princesses Elizabeth and Margaret. On 25th September 1955 the London Palladium turned to the still new medium of television for the legendary *Sunday Night at the London Palladium*, the first show featuring Gracie Fields. In 1958 an unknown entertainer called Bruce Forsyth was brought from a small venue in Eastbourne to host the show and built an audience of 28 million – half the

total population of Britain at the time. On one occasion in 1961, during an actors' strike, Sir Bruce Forsyth and Norman Wisdom carried the whole show themselves and earned widespread praise. In 1967 the show came to an end but the Palladium remains one of London's most popular venues and still hosts the Royal Variety Performance each year.

Pubs, pints and professors
London's drinking culture

Until 1950 brewing was one of London's major industries with hundreds of substantial breweries throughout the capital. There is now only one major brewery left – that of Fuller, Smith and Turner in Chiswick. All the others have moved out of town. Whitbread's Chiswell Street Brewery, opened in 1750, survives as a conference centre, beer having last been brewed there in 1976. But it is estimated that there are still about 7,000 pubs in London. In the 18th century, with a population one tenth of that which London now has, there were 15,000 drinking establishments, many of them selling gin to a population that used it to pacify querulous babies as well as to escape the realities of their lives. The drunkenness which was commonplace in Victorian Britain (not a phenomenon unique to the 21st century) led to the passing of licensing laws which regulated the numbers of pubs and their opening hours. These were further restricted during World War I when a story circulated that the disasters of the Battle of the Somme were due in part to a shortage of shells caused by excessive drinking by munitions workers. This was nonsense but a good story and led to the nationalisation of pubs near armaments factories, including pubs in Enfield where Lee-Enfield rifles were made. These were sold back to the private sector in 1922 though licensing laws of various degrees of restrictiveness have been a feature of pub life since.

Many of London's pubs have strange names which echo their histories. One of the busiest is the Prospect of Whitby in Wapping. This riverside pub, popular with sporting

teams as well as journalists, dates from 1520 when its association with pirates and smugglers earned it the name The Devil's Tavern. Nearby is Execution Dock where pirates and smugglers were hanged and their bodies left swinging from a gibbet for the duration of three tides. In 1777 its name was changed when a ship called the *Prospect*, registered at Whitby, was moored nearby. Samuel Pepys, Charles Dickens and JMW Turner were regular patrons.

The Prospect of Whitby

Another pub with sinister associations is the charming Lamb and Flag in Rose Street, Covent Garden. First recorded in 1623 it is one of central London's oldest pubs and was originally called The Bucket of Blood because of the prize-fights with which the Covent Garden area was associated well into the 18th century. The first official poet laureate, John Dryden, was attacked here in 1679 for writing scurrilous verses about one of Charles II's mistresses, the Duchess of Portsmouth. The pub has a bar named in Dryden's honour. Even older and more sinister is The Ostrich at Colnbrook, near Heathrow Airport (ironic given the non-flying species of bird). Dating from 1106 it owes its notoriety to a 17th-century landlord called Jarman and his wife whose hospitality extended to murdering and then robbing their guests by tipping them from their beds into a vat of liquid. They were caught when the body of their last victim, a wealthy merchant called Thomas Cole, was found in a nearby brook, thereby allegedly giving the area its name, Colnbrook.

Teetotal pub

Other pubs have gentler associations. The Mayflower, in Rotherhithe High Street, was built in about 1550 and known as The Shippe. In 1620 Captain Christopher Jones moored his vessel, the *Mayflower*, nearby before sailing for America with the Pilgrim Fathers, picking up passengers from Plymouth on the way and returning in subsequent years. In the 18th century it was rebuilt, supposedly incorporating timbers from the *Mayflower* in its structure. It was renamed The Spread Eagle and Crown but changed its name back to The Mayflower in 1957. It is very popular with American visitors and, because of its association with the USA, for many years it was the only place in the UK which sold American postage stamps.

Not far distant, in Greenwich, is The Trafalgar Tavern which opened in 1837 and quickly became a favourite meeting place for government ministers to enjoy dinners consisting of whitebait taken from the Thames. The last official Whitebait Dinner was celebrated by Gladstone's ministry in 1880 after which The Trafalgar went into decline. It was restored and reopened in 1968, complete with whitebait dinners (though not from the Thames, from which the fish had vanished). A dining club called Saints and Sinners, including some of Margaret Thatcher's ministers, resumed the habit of dining there.

The Anchor on Bankside dates from the 15th century and was almost certainly known to Shakespeare on account of its proximity to the Globe and other Elizabethan-era theatres. On 2nd September 1666 as the Great Fire of London gathered strength, Samuel Pepys visited the pub and 'staid till it was dark and saw the fire grow'. It also featured in the opening credits of the popular television series *Minder*. Perhaps the most unlikely pub name in London is The John Snow in Broadwick Street, off Carnaby Street in Soho. It stands close to the site of the former surgery of Dr John Snow who observed that people drawing water from a nearby well died of cholera and concluded that cholera was transmitted in polluted water. Few believed him at the time. John Snow would no doubt be alarmed to learn that he is commemorated

Dr John Snow

in a pub – by all accounts he was a strict teetotaller. Finally, The Princess Louise in High Holborn, named after Queen Victoria's fourth daughter, has been described as 'the most beautiful pub in Britain'. In 2007 it was thoroughly refurbished and returned to its full Victorian splendour with ornate plasterwork, gilt mirrors, decorated tiles and wood-panelled booths around an island bar. Prop up the bar and you're likely to be rubbing shoulders with thirsty professors from nearby London University and curators from the British Museum.

A LABOUR OF LOVE FOR LITTLE LEOPOLD

John Snow was also a pioneer in the use of anaesthetics. In 1853 he administered chloroform to Queen Victoria during the birth of Prince Leopold. Until that time doctors and clergymen (all men of course) had argued that labour pains were a punishment for Eve's transgression in the Garden of Eden. The Queen was delighted, describing the experience as 'soothing, quieting and delightful beyond measure' and declared that it should be available to all women in labour. The clergy and doctors were no match for Victoria and from that time anaesthetics became widely available for women in childbirth.

The Magnificent Seven
London's cemeteries

Some of London's most striking monuments are to be found in its cemeteries, many of which date from the early 19th century when London's churches could no longer accommodate further burials in their graveyards. As a result it was decided to build seven cemeteries around London: at Kensal Green (opened in 1832); West Norwood (1837); Highgate (1839); Abney Park, Nunhead and Brompton (1840); and Tower Hamlets (1841). They became known as the 'Magnificent Seven'. They were built by entrepreneurs who recognised that profits could be made from providing dignified burials for London's rapidly expanding population. Kensal Green Cemetery, which spans the borders of the London boroughs of Hammersmith and Fulham and Kensington and

West Norwood cemetery

Chelsea is older than Brookwood. It contains about 250,000 graves including those of Charles Babbage, mathematician and computer pioneer; Isambard Kingdom Brunel; and Marigold Frances Churchill, the daughter of Winston Churchill who died in 1921 aged three, the charming little monument to her by Eric Gill being Grade II listed in 2001. West Norwood, which is regarded by connoisseurs as having the finest monumental architecture of all London's cemeteries, has the graves of Paul Julius von Reuter who founded the famous news agency; Henry Tate the sugar magnate who funded the Tate Gallery; and Dr William Marsden who founded the Royal Free and Royal Marsden Hospitals.

Of the Magnificent Seven Highgate is probably the most famous simply because it contains the grave of Karl Marx though he shares the cemetery with the scientist Michael Faraday, the cricketer Frederick Lillywhite and Tom Sayers, the last bare-knuckle fighter, whose funeral was attended by 100,000 people and also by his huge dog whose effigy is carved on his tomb. Abney Park Cemetery in

Stoke Newington was particularly favoured by dissenters as it was built on land which had been the home of Isaac Watts, non-conformist hymn-writer, whose statue is a prominent feature in the grounds. It also contains the graves of William Booth, founder of the Salvation Army, his wife Catherine and of many Quakers who were active in the anti-slavery movement. Nunhead Cemetery in the borough of Southwark is the least well known of the Magnificent Seven and holds the grave of the bus pioneer Thomas Tilling, while beautiful Brompton Cemetery near Earl's Court is now managed by the Royal Parks and holds the graves of Sir Henry Cole (the driving force behind the 1851 Great Exhibition); shipping magnate Samuel Cunard; the militant suffragette Emmeline Pankhurst; and the journalist Bernard Levin. The last of the Magnificent Seven to be built, Tower Hamlets Cemetery is near Mile End station. Closed to burials since 1966 it is now a nature reserve and has acquired for this purpose the adjacent and indelicately named Scrapyard Meadow! The graves are mostly those of local residents including victims of London's last cholera epidemic which devastated a small area of Mile End in 1866, together with that of a local doctor, Rees Ralph Llewellyn, who carried out the autopsy on Mary Ann Nichols, the first victim of Jack the Ripper. It also contains the graves of victims of the wartime Bethnal Green disaster.

A memorial to the victims of the Bethnal Green Disaster

THE BETHNAL GREEN DISASTER

On 3rd March 1943 Bethnal Green Underground Station was the scene of Britain's worst civilian disaster of World War II when, for reasons that remain unclear, an orderly queue of people waiting to use the station as an air raid shelter surged forward on the stairway and 173 people were killed in the resulting crush. News of the tragedy was kept from the public at the time for morale purposes. Today a plaque at the station commemorates the tragic event.

The cemetery of Friends

Bunhill Fields cemetery, off the City Road in London, is not one of the Magnificent Seven but was used to bury cartloads of bones from St Paul's churchyard as early as 1549. In 1665 the Corporation of London enclosed the cemetery with a wall, intending to use it as a burial ground for victims of the Great Plague though it appears to have been used for ordinary burials too. The last burial was in 1854 but in the meantime it became popular with Non-conformists and was known as 'The Cemetery of Puritan England'. John Bunyan, Daniel Defoe, William Blake, the mother of the Methodist John Wesley and two members of the Cromwell family are buried here. The adjoining burial ground was purchased by Quakers in 1661, the first land they owned in London. It contains thousands of Quaker graves including that of the founder of the movement, George Fox.

INDEX

Amazing and Extraordinary Facts: The English Countryside
Ruth Binney
ISBN: 978-1-910821-01-5

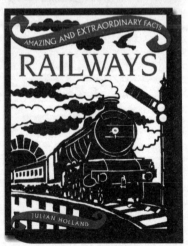

Amazing and Extraordinary Facts: Railways
Julian Holland
ISBN: 978-1-910821-00-8